Disability and Accessibility in the Music Classroom

Disability and Accessibility in the Music Classroom provides college music history instructors with a concise guide on how to create an accessible and inclusive classroom environment.

In addition to providing a concise overview of disability studies, highlighting definitions, theories, and national and international policies related to disability, this book offers practical applications for implementing accessibility measures in the music history classroom. The latter half of this text provides case studies of well-known disabled composers and musicians from the Western Art Music canon from the Middle Ages to the Twentieth Century as well as popular music genres, such as the blues, jazz, R&B, pop, country, and hip hop. These examples provide opportunities to integrate discussions of disability into a standard music history curriculum.

Alexandria Carrico is Assistant Professor of Music History at the University of South Carolina, Columbia.

Katherine Grennell is Senior Education and Training Specialist and Anthology Lecturer of History instructor at Buffalo State College.

Modern Musicology and the College Classroom
Series Editor: James A. Davis, SUNY Fredonia

Modern Musicology and the College Classroom is a series of professional titles for current and future college instructors of musicology in its broadest definition—encompassing music history, ethnomusicology, music theory, and music courses for all majors. Volumes feature a basic introduction to a significant field of current scholarship, a discussion of how the topic impacts pedagogical methodology and materials, and pragmatic suggestions for incorporating these ideas directly into the classroom.

Listening Across Borders
Musicology in the Global Classroom
Edited by James A. Davis and Christopher Lynch

Teaching Electronic Music
Cultural, Creative, and Analytical Perspectives
Edited by Blake Stevens

Race and Gender in the Western Music History Survey
A Teacher's Guide
Horace J. Maxile, Jr. and Kristen M. Turner

Music, Gender, and Sexuality Studies
A Teacher's Guide
Jacqueline Warwick

Disability and Accessibility in the Music Classroom
A Teacher's Guide
Alexandria Carrico and Katherine Grennell

Disability and Accessibility in the Music Classroom
A Teacher's Guide

**Alexandria Carrico and
Katherine Grennell**

NEW YORK AND LONDON

First published 2023
by Routledge
605 Third Avenue, New York, NY 10158

and by Routledge
4 Park Square, Milton Park, Abingdon, Oxon, OX14 4RN

Routledge is an imprint of the Taylor & Francis Group, an informa business

© 2023 Alexandria H. Carrico and Katherine Grennell

The right of Alexandria H. Carrico and Katherine Grennell to be identified as authors of this work has been asserted in accordance with sections 77 and 78 of the Copyright, Designs and Patents Act 1988.

All rights reserved. No part of this book may be reprinted or reproduced or utilised in any form or by any electronic, mechanical, or other means, now known or hereafter invented, including photocopying and recording, or in any information storage or retrieval system, without permission in writing from the publishers.

Trademark notice: Product or corporate names may be trademarks or registered trademarks, and are used only for identification and explanation without intent to infringe.

Library of Congress Cataloging-in-Publication Data
Names: Carrico, Alexandria, author.|Grennell, Katherine, author.
Title: Disability and accessibility in the music classroom: a teacher's guide / Alexandria Carrico and Katherine Grennell.
Description: [1.]|New York: Routledge, 2023.|Series: Modern musicology and the college classroom|Includes bibliographical references and index.
Identifiers: LCCN 2022023028 (print)|LCCN 2022023029 (ebook)|ISBN 9781032119366 (hardback)|ISBN 9781032119373 (paperback)|ISBN 9781003222224 (ebook)
Subjects: LCSH: Music--Instruction and study.|College students with disabilities--Education.|People with disabilities in music.|Musicians with disabilities.
Classification: LCC MT18.C307 2023 (print)|LCC MT18 (ebook)|DDC 780.71--dc23/eng/20220517
LC record available at https://lccn.loc.gov/2022023028
LC ebook record available at https://lccn.loc.gov/2022023029

ISBN: 9781032119366 (hbk)
ISBN: 9781032119373 (pbk)
ISBN: 9781003222224 (ebk)

DOI: 10.4324/9781003222224

Typeset in Times New Roman
by Deanta Global Publishing Services, Chennai, India

This book is dedicated to our students.

Contents

Acknowledgments   xi
Glossary   xiii

Introduction   1

Disability Inclusion *1*
The Purpose of This Book *2*
Chapter Overview *3*
Language and Positionality *4*
Notes *5*
References *6*

1 Contextualizing Disability Studies in the Music Classroom   8

Definitions and Models *8*
    Impairment and Disability *8*
    The Medical, Rehabilitation, and Social Models of
       Disability *9*
    Ableism and Disablism *10*
    Intersectionality *11*
History and Legislation *11*
Accessibility as Inclusion *13*
Notes *15*
References *16*

2 Accessible and Inclusive Applications in the Music Classroom 19

Universal Design for Learning 20
WCAG and Accessibility Checkers 22
Assessment 26
Course Design 29
Implementation and Engagement 35
Follow-Up Activities and Resources 39
Conclusion 40
Notes 41
References 43

3 Case Studies of Disabled Composers and Musicians in the Western Art Music Canon 45

The Middle Ages (400–1400) 46
   Zeitgeist and Institutions: Disability as Punishment or Divine Inspiration? 46
   Case Studies: Hildegard von Bingen and Francesco Landini 48
Additional Reading/Listening for Students 51
The Renaissance (1400–1600) 51
   Zeitgeist and Institutions: Humanism and Melancholia 51
   Case Studies: Gioseffo Zarlino and John Dowland 53
Additional Reading/Listening for Students 55
The Baroque (1600–1750) 55
   Zeitgeist and Institutions: The Doctrine of Affections and the Seconda Pratica 55
   Case studies: George Frideric Handel and Farinelli (Castrati) 56
Additional Reading/Listening for Students 60
The Classical Era (1750–1800) 60
   Zeitgeist and Institutions: The Enlightenment 60
   Case Studies: The Decline of Castrati and Disability in Haydn's Instrumentals Works 62
Additional Reading/Listening for Students 64
Romantic Era (1800–1900) 65

*Zeitgeist and Institutions: Medical Model of Disability,
   Statistics, and the "Norm" 65*
*Case studies: Ludwig van Beethoven and Robert
   Schumann 66*
Additional Reading/Listening for Students 70
Twentieth Century (1900–2000) 70
  *Zeitgeist and Institutions: Musical Modernism and the
   Social Model of Disability 70*
  *Case studies: Arnold Schoenberg, Igor Stravinksy, and
   Evelyn Glennie 72*
Additional Reading/Listening for Students 75
Conclusion 75
Notes 75
References 81

4 Case Studies of Disabled Composers and Musicians in Popular Music 86

The Blues 87
  *Case Studies: Blind Lemon Jefferson, Bessie Smith, and
   Amy Winehouse 88*
Additional Reading/Listening for Students 91
Jazz 91
  *Case Studies: Connie Boswell, Art Tatum, and Django
   Reinhardt 92*
Additional Reading/Listening for Students 96
Rhythm and Blues, Rock and Roll, and Pop Music 96
  *Case Studies: Ray Charles, Teddy Pendergrass, Britney
   Spears, and Lady Gaga 96*
Additional Reading/Listening for Students 101
Country 101
  *Case Studies: Hiram "Hank" Williams and
   Lil Nas X 103*
Additional Reading/Listening for Students 107
Hip Hop, Krip-Hop, and Dip Hop 107
  *Case Studies: Kenrick Lamar, Leroy Moore, and Warren
   "Wawa" Snipe 108*
Additional Reading/Listening for Students 110

Conclusion 110
Notes 111
References 116

Conclusion: Where Do We Go from Here?   121

Index   125

Acknowledgments

It has been a pleasure to work on this project. The lack of critical engagement with disability in most music courses combined with pervasive inaccessibility and ableism in academic environments necessitated the writing of this book. Yet, it was more than necessity that brought us to this project – it was the conversations with our students and colleagues about how we as educators and musicians can create a culture of care within the classroom that centers the disabled experience. This book is for those instructors and students. We owe you our deepest thanks.

Though the writing process was a collaborative one, it extended far beyond two co-authors. In fact, this book is the result of the work of many scholars and activists from the fields of music, history, law, religion, medicine, education, and philosophy. These resources have been absolutely invaluable in the writing of this book, and we are extremely grateful to all authors included in our References section. We would especially like to thank the members of the Disability and Deaf Studies Special Interests Groups of the American Musicological Society, Society for Ethnomusicology, and Society for Music Theory – this book builds upon your groundbreaking scholarship and is made possible by your supportive spirits.

We are deeply indebted to our editor, Jim Davis, who believed in this project and counseled us every step of the way, our publisher, Constance Ditzel, who supported the writing of this book, and the anonymous reviewers, who provided feedback that helped us re-imagine a more meaningful text. We offer our special thanks to James Deaville, whose expertise and insight proved invaluable during the editing process.

Alexandria offers her deepest gratitude to her family for their support and love. To Bill for his unwavering belief, to Michelle for her passionate conversations about pedagogy and inclusion, to Michael for his generous listening, and to Victoria for her meticulous feedback and editing – I could not have done this without you.

Katie wishes to thank and acknowledge the support, love, and encouragement from her family and friends. To Mitch, for his steadfast conviction in me, to my in-laws, Mari and John, for watching the kids so I could work, to my mom, Mary, brother Kevin, and step-mom Rachelle, my biggest cheerleaders, and to my children, Charlotte and Jake, my brightest inspirations. I dedicate my efforts to this book in honor of my beloved father, David McMahon, my most favorite historian and bibliophile.

Glossary

This glossary includes succinct definitions for key terms, theories, legislative policies, and acronyms discussed throughout this text.

Ableism: discrimination or oppression of disabled people.
Accessibility: the ability for all people to equitably engage with spaces, technologies, services, devices, or environments regardless of race, class, disability, gender, or sexuality.
Americans with Disabilities Act (ADA): civil rights law passed in 1990, which prohibits discrimination against disabled people in all areas of public life, such as employment, transportation, public accommodations, public services, and resources.
Americans with Disabilities Amendments Act of 2008 (ADAAA): revised and expanded version of the original ADA which altered the definition of disability, drawing a distinction between disabled people and people regarded as having a disability.
BIPOC: acronym for Black, Indigenous, and People of Color.
Bodymind: indicating the interconnection between physical and mental well-being and the integration of the body and the mind as one entity.
Center for Teaching and Learning: centers within a college or university that provide pedagogical support and professional development opportunities for faculty and instructors.
Convention on the Rights of Persons with Disabilities (CRPD): 2006, first comprehensive human rights treaty attempted in the twenty-first century specifically designed to affirm and protect the rights and dignities of disabled individuals around the world.
Cultural disability studies: view that culturally constructed ideas of normativity shape interpretations of bodymind variation.
d/Deaf: the lowercase "d" refers to the physical condition of deafness, while the uppercase "D" denotes cultural Deafness, which includes a shared history and language in addition to the physical condition of deafness.

DEIB: refers to diversity, equity, inclusion, and belonging efforts in higher education.

Differentiated Instruction (DI): teaching approach that utilizes flexible groupings to support the needs of specific students.

Digital Accessibility: practice of removing barriers that prevent interaction with websites, digital tools, and technologies.

Disability: a collection of constructed ideas, perceptions, and discriminatory assumptions made about people living with impairment(s) caused by an inaccessible environment that does not accommodate one's impairment.

Disablism: institutional discrimination towards disabled individuals.

Disability Studies: interdisciplinary academic field that exposes the inequities disabled people historically and currently face.

Disability Rights Movement: emerged in the 1960s and 1970s in the disability community as a reaction to limited access to social and economic resources as a result of paternalistic legal policies entrenched in the medical model of disability.

Education for all Handicapped Children Act of 1975: law that addressed the exclusion of disabled children from public school by issuing regulations for protecting and meeting the educational needs of disabled infants, toddlers, and children. This has since been expanded through the Individuals with Disabilities Education Act.

Eugenics: the study of selecting and promoting specific hereditary traits to improve the human species while also eliminating genetic traits by limiting the reproduction of so-called "undesirable" people through forced sterilization, abortion, miscegenation laws, and genocide.

Inclusion: providing equal access to learning opportunities for those who are routinely marginalized for belonging to minority groups.

Individuals with Disabilities Education Act (IDEA): passed in 1990, legislation that legally guarantees all children with disabilities access to free appropriate public education in the least restrictive environment.

Impairment: underlying biological, medical, cognitive, or psychological condition caused by illness, injury, or birth, which restricts a person's ability to carry out "normal" everyday activities.

Intersectionality: a theory that argues interconnectedness of systems of oppression, such as racism, sexism, classism, and disablism, and how such identities are mutually reinforcing and compound experiences of oppression.

Madness: in the pre-Enlightenment period the term "mad" was a catch-all term used to describe non-normative mental states brought on by supernatural forces. This conception shifted in the nineteenth century with the emergence of the medical model of disability and was conceptualized as a form of disease located within the mind. In the late twentieth and twenty-first centuries, the term "mad" has been reclaimed by advocates in an attempt to challenge negative stereotypes surrounding issues of mental health.

Mad Pride Movement: identity rights movement that seeks to overturn negative stigma about mental health.

Medical Model of Disability: emerged in the 1800s, conceptualizes disability exclusively as pathology by viewing impairment as a sickness in need of medical intervention and/or a cure.

Mental Health: refers to one's emotional, psychological, and social state.

Normative: refers to societally established expectations of typical bodies, minds, and behaviors. In Euro-American society, normativity is often defined as white, male, heterosexual, able-bodied.

Open Educational Resources (OER): publicly free and accessible educational resources, such as lesson plans and textbooks.

Screen Reader: assistive technology that allows visually impaired or blind users to read text and images on a computer screen with either a speech synthesizer or braille display.

Section 504: part of the Rehabilitation Act of 1973, designed to protect the rights of disabled people and prohibit discrimination from any program or activity receiving federal financial assistance.

Section 508: a 1998 Amendment to the Rehabilitation Act of 1973, requires Federal agencies to make all electronic and informational technology accessible to disabled people.

Social Model of Disability: posits that disability is the result of interactions between people living with impairments and an environment filled with physical, attitudinal, communication, and social barriers.

Student Disability Resource Center (SDRC): also known as the Accessibility Office or Student Accommodations Office, is a standalone center/office on campus that provides services and support for disabled students which can include accommodations, mediation, student workshops, training for instructors, etc.

Rehabilitative model of disability: stresses that the solution to eradicating the impairment is also through medical attention over a series of rehabilitative sessions.

Universal Design for Learning (UDL): a learning framework that provides instruction and suggestions for adapting classroom practices and teaching methods to meet the needs of all students.

Web Content Accessibility Guidelines (WCAG): a system developed by the World Wide Web Consortium that provides an international standard for accessibility for the creation and dissemination of web-based content.

Western Art Music Canon (WAM): written musical tradition of European and American music, colloquially labeled as "classical" music.

Introduction

As stated by disability studies scholar and advocate Tobin Siebers, disability is "the form of physical and mental diversity with the greatest potential for artistic representation."[1] Siebers argues that disabled people are important, yet undervalued creative agents whose artistic expression has much to teach us about culture. Despite this assertion, disabled people[2] are routinely marginalized and excluded from participating in the production of cultural knowledge, particularly in the arts and education. What do we miss through this erasure of the 15% of the world's population that identify as disabled?[3] To put it mildly – a great deal. In actuality, disabled people have always been crucial actors in the creation of culture, yet historical narratives constructed by non-disabled people often overlook these contributions, downplay experiences of disability, or fetishize disabled musicians as overcoming their disabilities through the arts. Such narratives are dangerous because they perpetuate the myth that unless a person with a disability is exceptionally talented or can serve as a source of inspiration for non-disabled people, they have little value.[4] While prevalent in all areas of society, these tropes are woven into the fabric of our educational systems and are embedded in how we teach music. In this book, we seek to contribute to overturning these narratives by providing instructors with a guide for creating a disability-inclusive music classroom through course design and curriculum.

Disability Inclusion

But what constitutes inclusion and how do we go about implementing these principles in the classroom? Shelley Moore, an inclusive-education consultant, states that, "Inclusive education relies on the diversity of its ecosystem to not only promote coexistence and tolerance, but to thrive on the learning and interaction of each person in the community."[5] As Moore suggests, diversity and inclusion are key components of creating a vibrant learning community. But how can instructors and professors of music teach it in a way that is both accessible and inclusive to an increasingly diverse student population? Many institutions are beginning to promote diversity, equity, inclusion, and belonging (DEIB) initiatives in order to address unequal access to resources and opportunities within systems of higher education. Yet, understandings of what constitutes diversity, equity, inclusion, and belonging, and the policies created to support these ideals, vary widely from institution to institution. Recently, DEIB has become synonymous with discussion of gender, race, and ethnicity. Notably missing from these identities is that of disability, which is an frequently overlooked yet essential and often intersecting identity.

Historically, disability has served as justification for excluding people from access to education, transportation, employment, healthcare, and even the right to live. As disability studies scholar Douglas Baynton states, "When categories of citizenship were questioned, challenged, and disrupted, disability was called on to clarify and define who deserved, and who was deservedly excluded from, citizenship."[6] While the concerns of disabled people have routinely been neglected in justice movements (women's suffrage, immigration, the Civil Rights Movement),[7] we argue that such experiences of marginalization and oppression are not competitive, but rather synergistic and mutually reinforcing.[8] To quote the wise words of Audre Lorde, "there is no hierarchy of oppression."[9] Increasingly, disability studies and the Disability Rights Movement have embraced this notion by engaging in intersectional scholarship and activism. As will be explored in Chapter 1, intersectionality, the interconnected nature of social identity categories and how they overlap to either create systems of privilege or marginalization,[10] is crucial to implementing practices of diversity, equity, inclusion, and belonging in education. Furthermore, intersectionality teaches us that making our classrooms accessible for students with disabilities also means addressing barriers to student success based on gender, sexual identity, race, ethnicity, class, age, and religion. Though important for many disciplines, discussions of intersectionality are particularly essential for understanding music, as it is a humanly constructed phenomenon that reflects the cultural values and identities of its makers. Thus, though this book specifically examines inclusion relative to disability, we will highlight the importance of intersecting identities and experiences throughout this text.

The Purpose of This Book

While there is a proliferation of resources and information available on accessible practices in the classroom, such as Universal Design for Learning and Differentiated Instruction, they are not situated specifically within the music classroom. Instructors face a myriad of challenges in designing and implementing music curricula. This is especially true for instructors who are seeking to expand conversations about representation and equity within the Western Art Music canon yet are unsure of how to make these changes. As junior academics who have been tasked with teaching large courses on music history and popular music and revising these curricula to address the gaps in representation, we understand the unrealistic expectations often placed on instructors to create an engaging and comprehensive course with little time. Thus, this book is designed to serve as a compact guide on how to make the music classroom more accessible and inclusive relative to disability in a way that is both manageable and digestible for instructors and meaningful for students. While many of the recommendations we suggest could be used for non-music classrooms, our intended audience for this text are the music history instructors at the collegiate level.

Chapter Overview

This book is divided into four chapters. Chapter 1 provides a concise overview of disability studies, highlighting definitions, theories, and national and international policies related to disability and centering these concepts within discussions of accessibility, inclusivity, intersectionality, and Disability Justice. Chapter 2 couches discussions of accessibility and inclusivity in relation to the music classroom. The primary goal of this chapter is to offer instructors tangible tools that allow them to cultivate inclusive pedagogical practices by addressing two main topics: (1) broad pedagogical perspectives related to disability and (2) specific applications to disability and accessibility in the music classroom. This will include discussions of teaching frameworks such as Universal Design for Learning, accessibility checker tools and the Web Content Accessibility Guidelines (WCAG), recommendations for course design, classroom engagement, accessible and student-centered assessments, and additional resources that engender multimodal ways of listening to, understanding, and processing music. Chapters 3 and 4 provide case studies of disabled composers and musicians as well as works that examine or embody disability that can be incorporated into curricula. Chapter 3 specifically examines disabled composers from the Western Art Music canon (WAM) from the Middle Ages to the twentieth century. The case studies selected for this chapter primarily feature well-known composers and musicians from the canon that are represented in most music history textbooks. This provides instructors the opportunity to incorporate discussions of disability into their teaching of composers and works that are already part of the curriculum. Similarly, Chapter 4 focuses on renowned disabled composers and musicians within various popular music genres, such as the blues, jazz, R&B, pop, country, and hip hop. In addition to exploring the lives and works of disabled musicians, we also explore the role of the music industry in creating disabling environments for artists. This chapter is not only useful for instructors focusing on vernacular genres, but is also important for those teaching Western canon classes exploring the musical landscape in the nineteenth- through twenty-first centuries, which increasingly incorporated popular genres such as the blues and jazz into European and American art music.[11]

Language and Positionality

Currently, there are two primary models that govern language surrounding disability and identity. The first is person-first language (person with disability), which emphasizes the personhood of the individual over their disability. This paradigm is often used within the realm of Special Education and is still preferred by some members of the disability community. The second model is identity-first language (disabled person), which asserts that disability is an essential aspect of one's identity and, furthermore, that there is nothing wrong with being disabled. There has been an increasing preference for identity-first language within the Disability Rights Movement and various disabled self-advocate communities.[12] As such, we use identity-first language throughout this text. However, we want to emphasize that it is best practice to defer to the linguistic preference of the person with whom you are communicating, understanding that disability is not a monolith and there is great diversity within the disability community.

As the authors of a book about music education and disability, we believe it is important to discuss both our positionality and our privilege within the disability community. Both of us live with multiple impairments and identify as disabled.

Like many, Katie Grennell's disability narrative is multilayered and serpentine. She was born with neuropathy in her left leg, which caused a foot drop and necessitates her need to wear an orthotic brace. Additional impairments resulted from the neuropathy, and while attending graduate school she developed chronic migraine and vertigo. This aggregation of several impairments, both visible and invisible, has complicated her continuous disclosure process in virtually all contexts. But at the risk of personifying inspiration porn,[13] Grennell's experience as a disabled woman has also given her unique vantage points from which to view the socially constructed world in which we live.

Alexandria (Alex) Carrico's impairment is invisible in nature and as a result she often unintentionally "passes"[14] for non-disabled. Though this ability to "pass" constitutes considerable privilege, it has also complicated the issue of disclosure in several ways. Firstly, since her disability is not visible, she often runs the risk of people questioning whether she really is disabled and searching for "proof"; secondly, within the disability community, she often worries that she will be rejected for not seeming "disabled enough" unless she is in the midst of a flare up; and finally, within academia, disclosure of mental illness, particularly as a junior faculty member, has the potential to compromise her ability to achieve tenure and promotion. It is important to note that the latter concern is not a comment on Carrico's specific institution, where she has the benefit of supportive colleagues and administrators, but rather is indicative of the ableist culture of institutions of higher education in general.[15]

Though only part of our identity, our impairments and connection to disability studies have shaped every facet of our lives. It has affected the support we need in order to fulfill our responsibilities as employees, educators, and family members; it has impacted the kind of advocacy-based research we engage in; and it has also deeply shaped the ways in which we connect with our students. While being disabled has presented many challenges, as highly educated white women from middle-class backgrounds, we possess enormous privilege. As such, we believe it is our responsibility to utilize this privilege to advocate and make space for disabled black, brown, indigenous, and LGBTQ people in our classrooms, our institutions, and our society. This means going beyond performative acts of inclusion and instead working towards long-term and lasting change.

In this book, we argue that such steps towards meaningful transformation of the classroom are possible by reexamining our methods of knowledge production. Who and what we study in the music classroom sends a message about who is worthy of our attention and, moreover, who can and should participate in the creation of culture. Therefore, rather than providing a series of "accessibility boxes" that need to be checked, we hope this book will serve to foster ongoing conversation and dialogue about the role of disability in music and society. In this way, *Disability and Accessibility in the Music Classroom: A Teacher's Guide* is not an ending point; it is a beginning that invites the reader to view disability as an essential component of accessibility and inclusion in music education.

Notes

1 Tobin Siebers, *Disability Aesthetics* (Ann Arbor, MI: The University of Michigan Press, 2012), 139.
2 Throughout this text, we will use identity-first language. For further explanation, see the "Language and Positionality" subsection below.

3 "Disability Inclusion," The World Bank, accessed February 2, 2022, https://www.worldbank.org/en/topic/disability#1.
4 Katie Ellis, *Disability and Popular Culture: Focusing Passion, Creating Community and Expressing Defiance* (Farnham: Routledge, 2015), 150.
5 Shelley Moore, *One without the Other: Stories of Unity through Diversity and Inclusion* (Winnipeg, MB: Portage & Main Press, 2016), 6.
6 Douglas C. Baynton, "Disability and the Justification of Inequality in American History," in *The Disability Studies Reader*, 4th edition, ed. Lennard J. Davis (New York: Routledge, 2013), 17.
7 Baynton, "Disability and the Justification of Inequality," 17.
8 Michael Rothberg, *Multidirectional Memory: Remembering the Holocaust in the Age of Decolonization* (Stanford, CA: Stanford University Press, 2009).
9 Audre Lorde, "There Is No Hierarchy of Oppression," *Bulletin: Homophobia and Education,* Council on Interracial Books for Children, 1983.
10 Kimberlé Crenshaw, "Demarginailzing the Intersection of Race and Sex: A Black Feminist Critique of Antidiscrimination Doctrine, Feminist Theory and Antiracist Politics," *University of Chicago Legal Forum* 1, no. 8 (1989), 139–167.
11 This is evident from the works of William Grant Still, such as *Afro-American Symphony*, as well as in the compositions of European composers such as Darius Milhaud and his *La creation du monde*.
12 Identity-first language is often preferred within Autistic self-advocate communities. See Jim Sinclair, "Why I Dislike Person-First Language," in *Loud Hands: Autistic People, Speaking*, edited by Julia Bascom, 23–24, (Washington, DC: The Autistic Press/The Autistic Self Advocacy Network, 2012).
13 Katie Ellis defines Inspiration porn as "where images of people with disability are constructed as inspirational in order to make the non-disabled feel better about themselves." Ellis, *Disability and Popular Culture*, 150.
14 Erving Goffman, *Stigma: Notes on the Management of Spoiled Identity* (New York: Simon & Schuster, Inc., 1963), 42.
15 For further discussion on ableism in academic institutions, see Jay Dolmage's text, *Academic Ableism: Disability and Higher Education.*

References

Baynton, Douglas C. "Disability and the Justification of Inequality in American History." In *The Disability Studies Reader*, 4th edition, edited by Lennard J. Davis, 17–33. New York: Routledge, 2013.
Crenshaw, Kimberlé. "Demarginailzing the Intersection of Race and Sex: A Black Feminist Critique of Antidiscrimination Doctrine, Feminist Theory and Antiracist Politics." *University of Chicago Legal Forum* 1, no. 8 (1989): 139–167.
Dolmage, Jay Timothy. *Academic Ableism: Disability and Higher Education*. Ann Arbor, MI: University of Michigan Press, 2017.
Ellis, Katie. *Disability and Popular Culture: Focusing Passion, Creating Community and Expressing Defiance*. Farnham: Routledge, 2015.
Goffman, Erving. *Stigma: Notes on the Management of Spoiled Identity*. New York: Simon & Schuster, Inc., 1963.

Lorde, Audre. "There Is No Hierarchy of Oppression." *Bulletin: Homophobia and Education*. New York: Council on Interracial Books for Children, 1983.

Moore, Shelley. *One without the Other: Stories of Unity through Diversity and Inclusion*. Winnipeg, MB: Portage & Main Press, 2016.

Rothberg, Michael. *Multidirectional Memory: Remembering the Holocaust in the Age of Decolonization*. Stanford, CA: Stanford University Press, 2009.

Siebers, Tobin. *Disability Aesthetics*. Ann Arbor, MI: The University of Michigan Press, 2012.

Sinclair, Jim. "Why I Dislike Person-First Language." In *Loud Hands: Autistic People, Speaking*, edited by Julia Bascom, 23–24. Washington, DC: The Autistic Press/The Autistic Self Advocacy Network, 2012.

The World Bank. "Disability Inclusion." Accessed February 2, 2022. https://www.worldbank.org/en/topic/disability#1.

1 Contextualizing Disability Studies in the Music Classroom

Inclusivity broadly defined means providing equal access to learning opportunities for those who are routinely marginalized for belonging to minority groups. But how do we implement this in the music classroom for disabled students and those with intersecting identities? Creating an inclusive classroom not only relates to how we teach and what we teach but also to the philosophical foundations upon which we build our pedagogy. Thus, Chapter 1 aids instructors in cultivating an inclusive teaching practice that is informed by disability studies and disability justice. While one does not need to be a disability studies scholar to create an accessible music classroom, having a fundamental comprehension of the core definitions, principles, and models of this field is imperative. This chapter explains the differences between disability and impairment, touches on the social, medical, and rehabilitative models of disability, and elucidates the valuable distinction between ableism and disablism. We provide a brief overview of the history of disability studies and the Disability Rights Movement, focusing on legislation such as the Americans with Disabilities Act (1990) and the United Nations Congress on the Rights of Persons with Disabilities (2006). Finally, we contextualize these concepts within a pedagogical framework, focusing on multifaceted manifestations and implementations of accessibility in the music classroom.

Definitions and Models

Impairment and Disability

There are many ways to define disability.[1] The Americans with Disabilities Act (ADA) defines disability as

> a person who has a physical or mental impairment that substantially limits one or more major life activities. This includes people who have

a record of such an impairment, even if they do not currently have a disability. It also includes individuals who do not have a disability but are regarded as having a disability.[2]

This definition is specific to the legal protections granted to disabled individuals under the ADA. Here the distinction between the terms "impairment" and "disability" are paramount. An **impairment** is the underlying biological, medical, cognitive, or psychological condition caused by illness, injury, or birth that restricts a person's ability to carry out "normal" everyday activities.[3] From a disability studies perspective, disability is not the result of an impairment; rather, disability is caused by an inaccessible environment that does not accommodate one's impairment.[4] Seen through this lens, **disability** is a social construction. More specifically, it is a collection of constructed ideas, perceptions, and discriminatory assumptions made about people living with impairment(s). According to disability studies scholar and advocate Tobin Siebers, "Disability is not a physical or mental defect but a cultural and minority identity."[5]

The distinction between impairment, as the underlying condition, and disability, as the social construction, is thus critical to the field of disability studies. In this case, it is not the impairment that needs to be fixed, cured, or corrected, but rather how society views those living with impairments.

The Medical, Rehabilitation, and Social Models of Disability

Disability studies scholars posit that there are different models of disability that either support the notion of disability as a social construction or challenge it. The two primary models that are divided along this dichotomy are the medical and the social models of disability. The modern **medical model** emerged in the late 1800s and conceptualizes disability exclusively as pathology by viewing impairment as a sickness in need of medical intervention. A related paradigm that intersects with this medical model is the **rehabilitation model**, which stresses that the solution to eradicating impairment is also through medical attention over a series of rehabilitative sessions. In both models, disability is located in the body of an individual who is encouraged to eliminate the impairment through medical assistance. The issue with these paradigms is not that a person living with impairment(s) seeks medical attention – in fact, many disabled people do rely on medical interventions and care in order to increase their quality of life. Thus, it is important to note that we are not demonizing medicine or medical professionals. However, the problem is that these medicalized models reinforce the notion that having an impairment marks one as inferior. Furthermore, they put the onus of responsibility on the disabled individual to eliminate the impairment, as opposed to holding society accountable for creating an accessible environment for all people.

By contrast, disability studies centers the **social model**, which posits that disability is the result of interactions between people living with impairments and an environment filled with physical, attitudinal, communication, and social barriers. Ultimately, these obstacles must change to enable people living with impairments to participate in society on an equal basis with others. It is important to note that the social model does not dismiss the physical, mental, and emotional realities of an impairment, but rather "It seeks to change society in order to accommodate people living with impairment; it does not seek to change persons with impairment to accommodate society."[6] Overall, the social model advocates for the fact that disabled people have the right to full participation in society, regardless of their impairments.

The varying definitions of both impairment and disability raise questions as to what constitutes a restriction or what should be included under the spectrum of "normal everyday activities." Feminist scholar Susan Wendell illustrates the difficulty of defining such parameters stating, "Neither impairment nor disability can be defined purely in biomedical terms, because social arrangements and expectations make essential contributions to impairment and disability, and to their absence."[7] Thus, disability is created by both biological and social conditions. This interaction is vital in understanding disability as a social construct and impairment as a medical condition or illness that work in tandem with one another.

Applied within educational contexts, the social model of disability creates a more accessible environment for all students. This kind of accessibility not only requires us to shift our perception of disability and impairment, but to acknowledge and actively work against the socially and culturally constructed barriers that disenfranchise non-normative bodyminds[8] in order to cultivate a more inclusive classroom, community, and world.

Ableism and Disablism

It is only through such intentional efforts that we will succeed in combating the ableism that has been codified into our social, cultural, and artistic values. **Ableism** is the discrimination or oppression of disabled people. By favoring the able-bodied, or those without an impairment, ableism upholds the medical model of disability by insisting that the impairment needs to be corrected and ultimately, eradicated. To say that someone is ableist means that they favor the normative[9] body of those living without an impairment. **Disablism**, on the other hand, is "a set of assumptions (conscious or unconscious) and practices that promote the differential or unequal treatment of people because of actual or presumed disabilities."[10] Put more clearly, it is institutional discrimination towards disabled individuals.

Intersectionality

Though traditionally associated with disability, it is important to note that ableism is inextricably linked to other forms of oppression, such as racism, sexism, genderism, classism, and ageism. The interconnectedness of these systems highlights the importance of understanding **intersectionality**, a term coined by activist and lawyer Kimberlé Crenshaw in the late 1980s.[11] Crenshaw sought to demonstrate that an African American woman experienced dual discrimination due to her doubly marginalized racial and gender identities. According to Crenshaw, these identities were mutually reinforcing and served to compound experiences of oppression. Though originally presented within the context of race and gender, discussions of intersectionality have expanded to encompass all identity categories. Rather than reducing individuals to a series of labels, intersectionality seeks to explore the depth and overlap of identity categories.

Intersectionality has become a core component of the Disability Rights Movement and of arts-oriented disability groups, such as Sins Invalid, the disability justice-based performance project that centers the experiences of artists of color and LGBTQ/gender-variant artists.[12] In addition to fostering opportunities for disabled artists to develop their works, Sins Invalid is also dedicated to political education as evidenced through their "10 Principles of Disability Justice." These principles promote disability justice by centering intersectional voices and experiences; advocating for sustainable and anti-capitalist systems; and supporting cross-movement and cross-disability initiatives led by those most impacted.[13] In this way, Sins Invalid provides a model for how artists can utilize their intersectional identities and experiences to promote a more inclusive and equitable society through the arts and education.

History and Legislation

The concept of intersectionality is an important part of disability studies and the Disability Rights Movement. Alongside the development of disciplines such as gender studies, women's studies, and Latinx studies, disability studies exposes the inequities disabled people face in a space of academic and intellectual inquiry. Like any other field, disability studies is constantly evolving. For the sake of clarity, this guide uses Rosemarie Garland-Thomson's concept of **cultural disability studies** to contextualize the field in a way that specifically relates to the music classroom.[14]

This concept "understands and investigates disability as a cultural product, as a way of interpreting bodily variation and a social concept that widely influences our collective thinking and practices."[15] She argues that using disability to analyze forms of cultural production such as music, art, and literary studies can be considered in applying issues of race, gender, and sexuality to studies of popular culture. Therefore, in a cultural context, disability contributes to "ideological and social formations that affect all cultural products and material spaces in the social order."[16]

Though interconnected, disability studies emerged as an academic outgrowth of the Disability Rights Movement that took place in the United States and the United Kingdom in the 1970s. This movement was closely tied to the various sociopolitical movements for Civil Rights, Gay Rights, and Women's Rights that emerged in the 1960s. Much like other marginalized identity categories, the disability community argued that disabled people were treated as second-class citizens and were limited socially and economically by paternalistic legal policies entrenched in the medical model of disability.[17] As a result, disabled individuals regularly experienced (and still experience) discrimination in employment, transportation, education, and medicine.

One important piece of legislation that came out of this time period was Section 504 of the Rehabilitation Act of 1973.[18] This section was designed to protect the rights of disabled people and prohibit discrimination from any program or activity receiving federal financial assistance.[19] However, the unequal enforcement of this statute as well as the broad interpretation of who qualified as "disabled" led to the 504 Sit-Ins of 1977. Here members of the disability community occupied a government building in San Francisco in order to force legislators to sign regulations that would require local and national governmental agencies to adhere to Section 504. This legislation was later expanded through the addition of Section 508 in 1998 to provide equitable access to technology. In addition to focusing on issues of deinstitutionalization and independent living for disabled people,[20] the Disability Rights Movement also addressed access to educational resources for disabled children. Perhaps the most important piece of educational legislation developed during this time was the Education for all Handicapped Children Act of 1975. This law addressed the exclusion of disabled children from public school by issuing regulations for protecting and meeting the educational needs of disabled infants, toddlers, and children.[21]

Both Section 504 and the Education for all Handicapped Children Act of 1975 were later revised and expanded through the Americans with Disabilities Act (ADA) of 1990 and the Individuals with Disabilities Education Act (IDEA) of 1990. According to the IDEA, "all children with disabilities are entitled to a free appropriate public education to meet their unique needs and prepare them for further education, employment and independent living."[22] By contrast, the ADA is all-encompassing and "prohibits discrimination against individuals with disabilities in all areas of public life, including jobs, schools, transportation, and all public and private places that are open to the general public."[23] This act was later revised in 2008 (the American with Disabilities Amendments Act of 2008, often abbreviated as ADAAA) and significantly changed the definition of disability. According to Elizabeth Emens, "One of the ADA's boldest features was its equal treatment of actual disability and regarded-as disability. The ADAAA, by contrast, separates actual and regarded-as into two different groups, which are expressly entitled to different remedies."[24] Under the ADAAA, individuals who are regarded as having a disability do not have the same right to accommodations as those with disabilities. Thus, the ADAAA further restricts the definition of disability, limiting accommodations for those who have been categorized as having a "regarded as" disability.

In addition to these examples of disability legislation relative to the US, the United Nations has also made efforts to expand legal protections for disabled people on a global scale. This is most evident through the Convention on the Rights of Persons with Disabilities (CRPD) of 2006. This was the first comprehensive human rights treaty attempted in the twenty-first century and was specifically designed to protect the rights of disabled individuals around the world.[25]

Such wide-sweeping recommendations for recognizing and accommodating disability represent an essential development for the Disability Rights Movement. However, many of the original signatories of the Convention have yet to ratify these statues, including the United States. This unequal adoption of the CPRD as well as the shortcomings of the acts discussed in this section demonstrates that, while invaluable to the global Disability Rights Movement, legislation alone has not and will not create an accessible society for all.

Accessibility as Inclusion

Such historical context is essential for addressing issues of access and inclusivity in relation to disability within higher education as many of these institutions are bound by these legislative tenets. This is certainly true in the United States, where colleges and universities must comply with the ADA (1990) and ADAAA (2008) in order to meet accessibility requirements. However, like so many of the other theories discussed in this chapter, **accessibility** can mean different things depending on context. Generally speaking, accessibility means having access to different spaces, technologies, services, devices, or environments. More explicitly, "accessible means that individuals with disabilities are able to independently acquire the same information, engage in the same interactions, and enjoy the same services within the same timeframe as individuals without disabilities, with substantially equivalent ease of use."[26] Accessibility is often associated with physical access to tangible spaces, such as buildings, dorms, classrooms, bathrooms, and transportation. A few classic examples of this are providing ramps, elevators, and handicapped parking spaces to enhance accessibility for physically disabled people. But accessibility also extends beyond the physical spaces and into the digital landscape. To that end, **digital accessibility** "refers to the inclusive practice of removing barriers that prevent interaction with, or access to websites, digital tools and technologies, by people with disabilities."[27]

In addition to physical and digital accessibility measures, many institutions have a standard disability policy that offers accommodations to students through a **Student Disability Resource Center (SDRC)**. While these centers are certainly helpful and we encourage instructors to become familiar with the one at your institution, their services are often limited to students who choose to disclose their disabilities. The issue is that the act of disclosure itself presents many challenges to inclusion and access. For instance, in order to gain accommodations through an SDRC, students must provide medical documentation that confirms their impairment and states what accommodations they need. However, not every student has access to medical care nor can they afford to undergo testing for disability diagnosis. In addition to economic hardship, disclosure can also create emotional and social barriers for students. Some students choose not to disclose their disabilities due to previous experiences of stigma or trauma, and, in the case of students with invisible disabilities, disbelief that the student is actually impaired. Each time a person with a disability discloses, they expose themselves to potential rejection and marginalization. The process of "coming out" as disabled is one that disabled people engage in continuously throughout their lives. Depending upon previous reception, one might either associate disclosure with empowerment of having their identity recognized or trauma if they are stigmatized.

We offer this analysis of "accessibility" in the context of higher education not to diminish the important resources that have been put in place for disabled students but to demonstrate the limitations of these systems. In fact, accessibility itself is often defined by the tenets of the aforementioned legislative acts, despite their notable shortcomings in terms of recognizing impairment. What does this mean for accessibility in your classroom? We argue that though institutions use this legislation to set standards for accessibility and inclusivity, these laws constitute the bare minimum of what we can and should do to accommodate our students. For instance, how might we create an inclusive learning environment by asking students what accommodations would help them be most successful in the classroom, rather than requiring them to go through official channels in order to implement baseline accessibility measures? Rather than retrofitting resources, we argue that in order to create a truly inclusive learning environment for disabled students, we must design courses that are accessible before the students ever enter the classroom. The following chapter will explore how to implement these accessibility measures in music course design through the principles of Universal Design for Learning (UDL) and in-person and digital accessibility efforts.

Notes

1 Language surrounding disability is constantly shifting as we learn more about impairment and the lived experiences of disabled individuals. As such, terminology is subject to change with cultural trends.
2 "What is the Definition of Disability under the ADA?" ADA National Network, last modified January 2022, https://adata.org/faq/what-definition-disability-under-ada.
3 Ibid.
4 Though impairment is often reductively viewed as the material aspect of disability, scholars have begun to argue that impairment is also socially constructed. See Jonathan Stern's *Diminished Faculties: A Political Phenomenology of Impairment* (2022).
5 Tobin Siebers, *Disability Theory* (Ann Arbor, MI: University of Michigan Press, 2008), 4.
6 "Social Model of Disability," People with Disability Australia, last modified 2018, https://pwd.org.au/resources/disability-info/social-model-of-disability/.
7 Susan Wendell, *The Rejected Body: Feminist Philosophical Reflections on Disability* (New York: Routledge, 1998), 35.
8 By "non-normative bodyminds" we refer to those who fall outside of societally expected physical, mental, and emotional standards.
9 "Normative" refers to societally established expectations of typical bodies, minds, and behaviors.
10 Kumari Fiona Campbell, *Contours of Ableism: The Production of Disability and Abledness* (London: Palgrave Macmillan, 2009), 6.
11 Kimberlé Crenshaw, "Demarginailzing the Intersection of Race and Sex: A Black Feminist Critique of Antidiscrimination Doctrine, Feminist Theory and Antiracist Politics," *University of Chicago Legal Forum* 1, no. 8 (1989), 139–167.
12 "Mission and Values," Sins Invalid, accessed January 13, 2022, https://www.sinsinvalid.org/mission.
13 "10 Principles of Disability Justice," Sins Invalid, accessed January 13, 2022, https://www.sinsinvalid.org/blog/10-principles-of-disability-justice.
14 We use Garland-Thomson's concept of cultural disability studies because it is still the basis on which many interdisciplinary research studies related to disability have been built.

15 Rosemarie Garland-Thomson, "Foreword," in *Sounding Off: Theorizing Disability in Music*, eds. Neil Lerner and Joseph N. Straus (New York: Routledge, 2006), xiv.
16 Garland-Thomson, "Forward," xiv.
17 Kitty Cone, "Short History of the 504 Sit-In," Disability Rights Education and Defense Fund, accessed December 15, 2021, https://dredf.org/504-sit-in-20th-anniversary/short-history-of-the-504-sit-in/.
18 The documentary *Crip Camp* provides a deeper exploration of the 504 Sit-Ins as well as the development of community ties in the Disability Rights Movement.
19 "A Guide to Disability Rights Law," U.S. Department of Justice, last modified February 2020, https://www.ada.gov/cguide.htm.
20 Doris Fleischer and Frieda Zames, *The Disability Rights Movement: From Charity to Confrontation* (Philadelphia, PA: Temple University Press, 2001), 33.
21 "A History of the Individuals with Disabilities Education Act," IDEA, last modified November 24, 2020, https://sites.ed.gov/idea/IDEA-History.
22 "Individuals with Disabilities Education Act (IDEA)," American Psychological Association, accessed December 15, 2021, https://www.apa.org/advocacy/education/idea.
23 "What is the Americans with Disabilities Act (ADA?)," ADA National Network: Information, Guidance, and Training on the Americans with Disabilities Act, last modified January 2022, https://adata.org/learn-about-ada.
24 Elizabeth F. Emens, "Disabling Attitudes: U.S. Disability Law and the ADA Amendments Act," in *The Disability Studies Reader*, 4th edition, ed. Lennard J. Davis (New York: Routledge, 2013), 46.
25 "Convention on the Rights of Persons with Disabilities (CPRD)," United Nations, last modified January 2, 2022, https://www.un.org/development/desa/disabilities/convention-on-the-rights-of-persons-with-disabilities.html.
26 "EITA Policy and Procedures," University of Montana's Office of Accessibility, accessed April 12, 2022, https://www.umt.edu/accessibility/implementation/policy/default.php#:~:text=%22Accessible%E2%80%9D%20means%20that%20individuals%20with,substantially%20equivalent%20ease%20of%20use.
27 "Digital Accessibility," Georgetown Law Office of Information Systems Technology, accessed April 12, 2022, https://www.law.georgetown.edu/your-life-career/campus-services/information-systems-technology/digital-accessibility/#:~:text=Digital%20accessibility%20refers%20to%20the,technologies%2C%20by%20people%20with%20disabilities.

References

ADA National Network: Information, Guidance, and Training on the Americans with Disabilities Act. "What is the Americans with Disabilities Act (ADA?)." Last modified January 2022. https://adata.org/learn-about-ada.

———. "What is the Definition of Disability under the ADA?" Last modified January 2022. https://adata.org/faq/what-definition-disability-under-ada.

American Psychological Association. "Individuals with Disabilities Education Act (IDEA)." Accessed December 15, 2021. https://www.apa.org/advocacy/education/idea.

Campbell, Fiona Kumari. *Contours of Ableism: The Production of Disability and Abledness.* London: Palgrave Macmillan, 2009.

Cone, Kitty. "Short History of the 504 Sit-In." Disability Rights Education and Defense Fund. Accessed December 15, 2021. https://dredf.org/504-sit-in-20th-anniversary/short-history-of-the-504-sit-in/.

Crenshaw, Kimberlé. "Demarginailzing the Intersection of Race and Sex: A Black Feminist Critique of Antidiscrimination Doctrine, Feminist Theory and Antiracist Politics." *University of Chicago Legal Forum* 1, no. 8 (1989): 139–167. http://chicagounbound.uchicago.edu/uclf/vol1989/iss1/8.

Dolmage, Jay Timothy. *Academic Ableism: Disability and Higher Education.* Ann Arbor, MI: University of Michigan Press, 2017.

Emens, Elizabeth F. "Disabling Attitudes: U.S. Disability Law and the ADA Amendments Act." In *The Disability Studies Reader*, 4th edition, edited by Lennard J. Davis, 42–57. New York: Routledge, 2013.

Fleischer, Doris Zames and Frieda Zames. *The Disability Rights Movement: From Charity to Confrontation.* Philadelphia, PA: Temple University Press, 2001.

Garland-Thomson, Rosemarie. "Forward." In *Sounding Off: Theorizing Disability in Music*, edited by Neil Lerner and Joseph N. Straus, xiii. New York: Routledge, 2006.

Georgetown Law Office of Information Systems Technology. "Digital Accessibility." Accessed April 12, 2022. https://www.law.georgetown.edu/your-life-career/campus-services/information-systems-technology/digital-accessibility/#:~:text=Digital%20accessibility%20refers%20to%20the,technologies%2C%20by%20people%20with%20disabilities.

Hampton, Jameel. "The 1970 Chronically Sick and Disabled Persons Act: Fifty Years On." *Disability & Society* 35, no. 5 (2020): 831–836. DOI: 10.1080/09687599.2020.1751080.

IDEA. "A History of the Individuals with Disabilities Education Act." Last modified November 24, 2020. https://sites.ed.gov/idea/IDEA-History.

Lewis, Talila. "Ableism 2020: An Updated Definition." Last modified January 25, 2020. https://www.talilalewis.com/blog/ableism-2020-an-updated-definition.

Newnham, Nicole and Jim LeBrecht, dir. *Crip Camp.* Hunter, New York: Good Gravy Films. Netflix, 2020.

People with Disability Australia. "Social Model of Disability." Last modified 2018. https://pwd.org.au/resources/disability-info/social-model-of-disability/.

Shakespeare, Tom. "The Social Model of Disability." In *The Disability Studies Reader*, 4th edition, edited by Lennard J. Davis, 214–221. New York: Routledge, 2013.

Siebers, Tobin. *Disability Theory.* Ann Arbor, MI: University of Michigan Press, 2008.

Sins Invalid. "10 Principles of Disability Justice." Accessed January 13, 2022. https://www.sinsinvalid.org/blog/10-principles-of-disability-justice.

———. "Mission and Values." Accessed January 13, 2022. https://www.sinsinvalid.org/mission.

United Nations. "Convention on the Rights of Persons with Disabilities (CPRD)." Last modified January 2, 2022. https://www.un.org/development/desa/disabilities/convention-on-the-rights-of-persons-with-disabilities.html.

University of Montana, Office of Accessibility. "EITA Policy and Procedures." Accessed April 12, 2022. https://www.umt.edu/accessibility/implementation/policy/default.php#:~:text=%22Accessible%E2%80%9D%20means%20that%20individuals%20with,substantially%20equivalent%20ease%20of%20use.

U.S. Department of Justice. "A Guide to Disability Rights Law." Last modified February 2020. https://www.ada.gov/cguide.htm

Wendell, Susan. *The Rejected Body: Feminist Philosophical Reflections on Disability*. New York: Routledge, 1998.

2 Accessible and Inclusive Applications in the Music Classroom

Part of creating an accessible environment is understanding your students' current skill set, their intersectional experiences, and their needs in order to tailor the course to them instead of trying to fit them into the course. Though this is a pedagogical concept that could be applied to any course, it is especially important when attempting to aid students in honing their musical communication skills. Musical communication entails not only understanding the structure and aesthetic characteristics of specific styles and genres, but also knowing how to utilize this knowledge to connect with their students or audiences. By centering the experiences and values of your students as a point of departure for knowledge production, you are empowering them to take ownership of the learning process and to become co-creators of musical meaning and culture. Musical communication is a skill they will utilize throughout their careers, whether they are music educators or practitioners.

Overall, Chapter 2 challenges instructors to commit to making inclusive practices part of their teaching philosophy while simultaneously offering the tools and support to demystify the practice of accessibility. This will help shift conceptions of accommodation as an additional burden for instructors and instead instill a culture rooted in accessibility. While both the shift in approach and application of strategies will require work on the part of the instructor, we aim to reduce the amount of labor by making the process more manageable and digestible. With this chapter, we provide instructors with the tools to make accessibility and inclusivity a central aspect of their pedagogy that will serve them beyond the scope of a single class.[1]

Though several overarching ideas, such as Universal Design for Learning, could certainly apply to any classroom setting, this section will couch discussions of accessibility and inclusivity in relation to the music classroom. The primary goal of this chapter is to offer instructors tangible tools and suggestions that will allow you to cultivate inclusive pedagogical practices by addressing two main topics: (1) broad pedagogical perspectives related to disability and accessibility, and (2) specific approaches and applications to disability and accessibility in the music history classroom. We begin by discussing the principles of Universal Design for Learning (UDL) as our recommended pedagogical framework. Before moving on to the three main sections of the chapter, we examine the Web Content Accessibility Guidelines (WCAG) as well as the accessibility checkers available in some of the more frequently used tools by instructors (i.e. Microsoft and Adobe Acrobat). These categories will then be contextualized through tangible suggestions specific to the music classroom organized into the following four sections: (1) assessment, (2) course design, (3) implementation and classroom engagement, and (4) follow-up resources and activities. Each of these stages emphasize the importance of engendering multimodal ways of hearing, listening, and processing music. Unlike the other chapters in the book, here we directly address instructors using "you" or "your" as this section is focused on applications for accessibility and implementation strategies.

Universal Design for Learning

In terms of accessibility and learning paradigms, Universal Design for Learning (often abbreviated as UDL and occasionally called Universal Design in Education or Universal Design of Instruction) is the most commonly referenced and used. Defined as "a framework to improve and optimize teaching and learning for all people based on scientific insights into how humans learn,"[2] UDL was designed to effectively reach *all* students, wherever they may be on their educational journey by providing instruction and suggestions for adapting classroom practices and teaching methods to meet the needs of all students, particularly the outside pins, to borrow from Shelley Moore. Using bowling as a metaphor for inclusive teaching, Moore stresses the importance of teaching to the "outside pins." The strategy typically used by professional bowlers is to hit the outside pins as it increases the probability of knocking down all other pins. But yet in teaching, we often aim for the student that has everything – the headpin.

> Classrooms have changed-for the better, I think-but our education system still hasn't. Why aren't we teaching to the kids who are the hardest to reach? Why aren't we looking for the kids who have hoodies over their heads and headphones in their ears, who probably didn't sleep much and may be hungry, or even looking to the child who has autism as our starting point-and aim?[3]

The UDL Guidelines provide instruction and suggestions for adapting the classroom/teaching methods to meet the needs of the outside pins, which in turn benefits all remaining pins.

More on the research and structure behind UDL, "UDL is intended to enhance access to learning by reducing physical, cognitive, intellectual, and organizational barriers and other obstacles to learning. UDL principles also lend themselves to the implementation of inclusionary practices in the classroom."[4] Anne Meyer and David Rose, the minds behind UDL, structured their framework into three different principles, each corresponding to a different portion of the brain that impacts learning: Engagement (The "Why" of Learning), Representation (The "What" of Learning), and Action and Expression (The "How" of Learning). Within each of these categories are guidelines with related checkpoints (access, build, internalize) that provide additional information and recommendations based on their relevant category.[5]

When contextualizing UDL for teachers, the dinner party analogy is often used. Katie Novak of Novak Education Consulting describes this analogy best. Let us say you are preparing for a dinner party with ten people. As host, you want to ensure that everyone has a great meal and dining experience. A UDL perspective would mean you anticipate and predict the variability of possible guests, even though you may not know their specific food preferences.[6] This could look like preparing a buffet of choices and options that engenders diversity by giving the autonomy to your guests to select a dish that resonates with them the most without having to ask for additional accommodations, such as preparing dishes that are vegetarian, vegan, meat-based, dairy-free, gluten-free, etc. In a similar way, giving learners control over their own choice empowers them by having them self-assess their needs to guide them in their decision. Within the context of a dinner party, this would mean they need to assess their food preferences or sensitivities, how hungry they are, what looks good, etc.[7]

While instructors need to be able to adapt during a class session to student questions or unforeseen obstacles in a planned class activity, it can be seen as contradictory to expect instructors to be flexible and agile in their teaching while also strategically planning ahead and staying organized. To avoid this, UDL guidelines are intended to be implemented as an instructor prepares for their course, not after the fact. It is much easier to take this approach at the outset of course planning than to retrofit the framework during or afterwards.[8] This might look like selecting a wide variety of readings available in various formats (i.e. audio book, large print, etc.), devising a diverse group of assessments (performances, listening quizzes, producing a podcast, etc.) to measure your students' learning, and teaching the content in a multitude of ways (traditional lecture, guest lecture or performance, listening to a podcast together as a class, etc.). In relation to the music classroom, under the representation principle, one of the perception checkpoint guidelines is to offer alternatives for auditory information. This could mean providing music recordings *before* class, offering noise canceling headphones (if available) to students during class, and providing lyrics and/or sheet music ahead of time.[9]

UDL is not the panacea to the ableism that continues to dominate higher education, nor is it often genuinely embraced or applied outside of the discipline of education. Disability Rights scholar Jay Dolmage states, "I believe that part of the ongoing problem with UD is that it is being checklist-ified, over-simplified, hollowed out, and torn apart from the actual, tricky, ongoing negotiations of classroom practice."[10] To avoid approaching UDL from a checklist standpoint that is rooted in compliance, Dolmage frames the suggestions as "places to start" that serve as an invitation to instructors as opposed to a to-do list. This invitation is not always viewed as such, and although Dolmage's essay was published in 2015, notions of the UDL as an oversimplified and hollowed-out approach to accessible learning still hold sway today. This compliance approach often leads to what Dolmage refers to as interest convergence, which is "the idea that conditions change for minorities only when the changes can be seen (and promoted) as positive for the majority of the group as well."[11] Our job as instructors makes this more difficult as we need to be mindful of how we approach UDL, how we address disability in our classes, and how we frame our own positionality to reaffirm our commitment to creating and sustaining an accessible and inclusive learning environment for our students.

WCAG and Accessibility Checkers

Considering the frequency with which higher education relies upon technology to deliver class content and materials, the need for web accessibility guidelines and checks are critical, bringing us to the WCAG. The

> Web Content Accessibility Guidelines (commonly abbreviated as WCAG) is developed through the W3C (World Wide Web Consortium) process in cooperation with individuals and organizations around the world, with a goal of providing a single shared standard for web content accessibility that meets the needs of individuals, organizations, and governments internationally.[12]

Simply put, the WCAG 2.1 serve as the international standard for accessibility and compliance with the Americans with Disabilities Act (ADA) for the creation and dissemination of web-based content.[13] While WCAG is by far the most comprehensive and widely recognized accessibility guidelines, it is not legally required that any entity, federal or not, creating web-based content adhere to these guidelines.[14] Although Section 508 was heavily influenced by the WCAG, they are not one and the same, and the WCAG are far more detailed, technical, and comprehensive.[15]

Accessible and Inclusive Applications 23

The WCAG are organized into the following categories: perceivable, operable, understandable, and robust.[16] The requirements are further divided into three separate levels of conformance: A, AA, and AAA. Level A is the bare-minimum of compliance, Level AA is the target compliance level that legally complies with the ADA, and Level AAA meaning the compliance efforts have exceeded the requirements.[17] Although we will not delve into each specific guideline, many of the recommendations and best practices presented in this section derive from the WCAG.

Accessibility Checkers: Understanding the complexities of the WCAG is no easy feat, nor is learning how to implement the guidelines. To help instructors provide accessible content that aligns with the WCAG without having to become experts themselves, there are accessibility checkers available in the most frequently used tools by instructors, such as Microsoft Word and PowerPoint, and Adobe Acrobat.[18] There are a significant number of accessibility checkers available, both for free and at a cost, to determine various aspects of accessibility, such as color contrast, HTML Markup code, website accessibility, and button contrast. More pertinent to higher education, the Learning Management System (LMS) Blackboard (now Anthology) offers Ally, an LMS-agnostic (meaning it is compatible with other LMS's other than Blackboard) accessibility tool fully integrated into your LMS to manage accessible learning content. For institutions that have Ally (it is not free), it is built right into the LMS so that instructors can remediate inaccessible content and allow students to select alternative formats for course content.[19]

Microsoft Accessibility Checker: Microsoft has an accessibility checker for each of its tools. Word and PowerPoint (PPT), two of the most frequently used Microsoft tools by instructors, have intuitive and helpful accessibility checkers that provide instructions on how to fix any issues detected. Before posting either a Word document or PPT in your LMS, run it through the accessibility checker. The Microsoft Accessibility checker will then identify all issues, point out where they are located in the document or PPT, and provide suggestions for how to fix them.[20] Below are some of the general tips and best practices to consider while creating content in either Word or PowerPoint.

- Use Alternative Text (Alt Text) to describe the meaning being conveyed in the image. This is critical for students with visual impairment who rely on screen readers. For images that are purely decorative, Alt Text is not necessary and can be marked as such.
- Do not use only color to convey meaning.
- If using bullet points, read in the order they are presented (for either recording or presentation purposes).

24 *Accessible and Inclusive Applications*

- Avoid memes; they are inaccessible.
- Use unique titles per PPT slide.
- Include text alongside images: When using an image, include text that accompanies it to provide necessary context.
- Describe images: For images that contribute to the meaning/context of that slide, describe the image and its significance when presenting or recording.
- Slide Order: Screen readers read the elements of a slide in the order they were added, which can misconstrue the meaning and intention behind the slide. The accessibility checker will detect slides that have potential problems with reading order.
- Hyperlinks: Describe the hyperlink that provides enough information and direction for students to access it.

Adobe Acrobat Pro Accessibility Checker: As of the writing of this book (2021–2022), Adobe Acrobat offers three different tools (with different versions): Acrobat Standard, Acrobat Pro DC, and Acrobat Reader. At a cost, users can edit, modify, and create new PDFs,[21] and more, in the various versions of Acrobat Standard and Acrobat Pro DC.[22] Acrobat Reader is free for all and allows users to view, comment, and print PDFs. Both Acrobat Standard and Acrobat Pro DC include an accessibility checker that provides a detailed report indicating areas of concern and steps to remediate, whereas Acrobat Reader does not. Admittedly more complicated than the accessibility checkers for Microsoft products, learning how to make your PDFs accessible will take some time. There are several strong training guides and training videos available for free on Adobe's website.[23] Adobe Acrobat also provides some additional and unique accessibility features, such as Reflow view, that will check the reading order of your PDF, Read Out loud, that allows the creator to use the text-to-speech conversion tool to experience the process, and the Reading Order tool that examines the reading order of the document.[24]

PDFs have a unique structure to them and as such warrant a different approach to ensuring they are accessible. Below you will find a concise list of common issues and/or things to keep in mind when either creating an accessible PDF or remediating an inaccessible PDF. The accessibility checker in Acrobat will review each of these items, but correctly addressing these common issues and/or considerations from the beginning will save you time in the long run. Additionally, it is important to note that even if you first create the resource in Word or any other Microsoft tool and it passes the accessibility checker, you will still need to run it through the Acrobat checker given the differing formats.

- **Logical Reading Order**: For students utilizing a screen reader, the PDF needs to be organized logically to ensure it is both contextual and accurate.
- **Tagging**: Tagging divides the content into various sections and provides logical reading order to the PDF. This is critical for students using screen readers or for those relying on the keyboard as opposed to a mouse to browse the PDF effectively. Some tag examples are headings, paragraphs, tables, etc. Auto-tagging is not always reliable; therefore, be sure to always run the accessibility checker.
- **Alternative Text (Alt Text)**: provides meaning and context to individual images.[25]
- **Color Contrast**: Colors must have adequate contrast between the text color and background color, including any text on images or icons, as it is necessary for students who are colorblind or have low contrast sensitivity. Running the accessibility checker in Adobe Acrobat will review that the color contrast in your document is sufficient, and if not, provide further information on how to fix it.[26]
- **Searchable text**: PDFs that contain a lot of images, logos, or icons can become barriers for students using assistive technology which can only be read as text. Making your PDF searchable will convert your image-rich PDFs into an accessible document. Adobe's **optical character recognition (OCR)** tool is "the conversion of images of text (scanned text) into editable characters, allowing you to search, correct, and copy the text."[27] One thing to bear in mind is that if the scanned object has any flaws, such as blurriness or brightness, the results may not be entirely accurate or comprehensible. The accuracy of OCR is entirely dependent on the quality and condition of your original object.
- **Title**: A unique title must be included and be meaningful/representative of the document to confirm that students using a screen reader are referencing the correct document. To add a title, open your file in Acrobat, click on file, and select properties from the menu. The description tab is where you can add the title.
- **Document Language**: To help screen readers discern text more easily (i.e. pronunciation rules and accurate closed captions), it is important to indicate the language of your document. Similar to adding a title, to specify which language your document is in, click on document properties, then on the Advanced tab, and select your language from the drop-down menu.
- **Bookmarks**: Particularly for long documents, including meaningful bookmarks can make it easier for students to navigate the various sections of the PDF.

- **Table of contents**: Including a Table of Contents provides students with a hierarchical overview of how the content is structured. It also allows them to navigate directly to a specific section of the document.
- **Page Numbers**: Include page numbers in the margins for more effective navigation.

Assessment

The assumption that all instructors and professors understand the complexities of pedagogy and assessment, in addition to having a natural ability to teach effectively, still pervades academia. Lack of exposure to *why* and *how* assessment is important, lack of inclusion on decisions related to measuring student learning, and a disengaged or negative view towards assessment often prohibits the constantly evolving dialogue/process that it could be. To adequately address the topic of assessment as it relates to efforts of creating an inclusive music history classroom, this section will be broken up into the following: writing learning outcomes, rubrics, formative assessment, accessibility and class climate surveys, selecting assignments, and reevaluating exam procedures.

Learning Outcomes guide the direction of your class. Most institutions have their own institutional, departmental, and student learning outcomes instructors are required to include in their syllabi. These may or may not align with your desired outcomes for the course, and if that is the case, why not add your own? While we are not suggesting avoidance of any institutional or departmental outcomes, we are asking you to consider including more specific learning outcomes for your class and even individual assignments. There are several different learning taxonomies,[28] such as Fink's *Taxonomy of Significant Learning* and Bloom's *Taxonomy of the Cognitive Brain* (Revised), that provide guidance on writing strong learning outcomes. Below are some suggestions and considerations for creating relevant and measurable learning outcomes.

- Limit to 3–5 outcomes at most.
- Begin each outcome with an action verb (i.e. action verbs associated with either taxonomy).
- Use one action verb per outcome (i.e. demonstrate, identify, create, construct, etc.).[29]
- Avoid vague verbs such as understand or know (they are not measurable).
- Keep the student in mind: what should they be able to do by the end of the activity, lesson, assignment, or course?

Rubrics: Rubrics are scoring guides that explicitly outline the expectations for each component of an assignment. While the creation of a rubric can be time-consuming at first, it will prove immensely helpful during grading, for both the students and the instructor.[30] Additionally, most LMS's include a rubrics tool, allowing instructors to directly embed them into assignments or assessments within the course shell. Check with the teaching and learning center or educational technology office as they will likely have resources available. Some institutions require their instructors to use a specific set of rubrics when assessing student work, so you will want to check if this is the case prior to creation. But whether you use your own rubrics or those mandated by your department and/or institution, it can be both helpful and empowering for students to understand their grade breakdown.

Selecting Assignments: Include a variety of assignments to address the diverse learning styles of your students and support an inclusive approach to assessment. While there are the more traditional assignments such as concert reviews, tests and quizzes, listening quizzes, class discussions, or album reviews (this list is not intended to be exhaustive), there are several alternative assignments to consider that can be modified to ensure accessibility and inclusivity in your music classroom.

- Video assignments: Flip, TikTok, Vlogs, and other free mediums are great alternatives to discussion boards. Instructors can provide prompts for students to respond to in their video posts and general guidelines to follow. Require students to provide closed captions and transcripts for accessibility purposes.
- Multimedia project: typically involves a variety of media, such as video, audio, text, images, sound, etc. Assigning this type of project will likely be for those instructors that have more experience with this, but it would make for an interesting and diverse approach to assessing your students' content comprehension.
- Original music creation
- Lyrical challenge: Have students select one of their favorite songs, with lyrics, and re-write the lyrics.
- Music video
- Community work
- Podcasts: Have students create a podcast related to the course content or assign a podcast throughout the duration of the semester and have students provide their responses to it, either as a journal entry, traditional paper, discussion board, or even video assignment.[31] Require students to provide transcripts for any video or audio assignments.

Formative assessment refers to a wide variety of methods used by instructors to conduct ongoing evaluations of student comprehension, learning needs, and academic progress during a class or activity to then allow for adjustments or modifications by the instructor. Because it is intended to observe student learning at the time to then provide ongoing feedback to instructors, the assessments themselves typically have low or no point value. Formative assessment guides the instructor in ensuring students' comprehension of the material and can reveal the need for more explanation, a study guide, or some other type of support resource. This is particularly important for disabled students and other marginalized groups who may otherwise remain silent about their learning needs. Below you will find some examples of formative assessment to consider using.

- **Surveys/quizzes**: Keep the number of questions short and focused on student comprehension of the content. This can be administered via your LMS, Google Forms, Survey Monkey, or any other free and available poll/survey tool. These surveys or quizzes should be of low or no point value.
- **One-Minute paper**: During class, give students one minute to answer a question or prompt. Questions should not be yes or no, as the intention is to get students to think critically about the content and their perception of their learning. Papers should not be graded, but can be used to determine further class activities, content, etc.
- **Peer review**: Pair students together to provide feedback on each other's work. Provide specific questions and tasks to be completed by each student during the peer review activity.
- **Muddiest Point**: Ask students to identify the most confusing part of a lecture as well as what was most clear.

Surveys: Consider administering two uniquely separate surveys throughout the semester. These surveys can be administered via the following free tools: Google forms, Survey Monkey, or the survey tool in your LMS. These surveys should be anonymous and that must be explicitly communicated with your students. To be administered at the beginning of the semester, an **accessibility survey** can be used to gauge the accessibility needs of students in terms of learning and logistics (computer access, Wi-Fi, etc.). We recommend connecting with either the educational technology office, accessibility office, or information technology office beforehand to familiarize yourself with any equipment or resources you can potentially provide to your students. Below are some sample questions.

- Do you know where to find accessibility resources for your campus?
- Do you have any accessibility concerns for this course?
- Do you have reliable internet and computer/tablet access at home?

- Do you have access to a webcam? Only ask this question if you intend to have students use their webcams for class activities or assignments.
- To help you experience the music we will discuss in this class, are there any specific technology tools you will require?

The **classroom climate** survey should be administered halfway through the semester to allow instruction time to make tweaks or modifications to class content, access to materials, and the overall classroom environment.[32] Below are some suggestions for questions to include.

- How is the pace of content? Too fast? Too slow?
- Are there too many words on PPT slides? Too few?
- Are we spending enough time on listening examples? Too much time?
- Are there any additional accessibility concerns you have related to this class?
- Have you felt included and valued in this class?

Exam considerations: One of the most common accommodation needs for students is extended test time. If possible, consider removing the time limit for all students for exams or quizzes as it could drastically reduce anxiety around test-taking for all students. In this vein, if students have historically completed their exams or quizzes in class, consider moving them online via the LMS. Not only could this free up class time, it would also be more convenient for students typically juggling heavy course loads, work, family commitments, and for those with impairments that hinder their ability to effectively or confidently take exams or quizzes. It is important to note that some institutions have strict guidelines when it comes to administering exams. If instructors do not have the ability to alter the time limit for exams, encourage students to pursue accommodations via the accessibility office on campus and provide them with the contact information.

Course Design

This section addresses how to design an inclusive music course by building an accessible infrastructure that sets students up for success before they even enter the classroom. Some of the topics discussed are creating the syllabus, setting up your course in your Learning Management System (LMS), and selecting accessible and diverse readings and music samples. Several of the suggestions provide an overview of general best practices that could be implemented in any course by utilizing the principles of UDL in the creation of syllabi, course policies, and assignments. However, we will also provide recommendations that specifically address accessibility concerns unique to the music classroom.

The syllabus: If we think about the syllabus as a blank canvas for a course, as instructors it is up to us to add in the color, shapes, words, and inspiration that will serve as the guidepost for students. It is here, before students even set foot in the classroom (either virtually or face-to-face) that the learning environment begins to take shape. It is also here that instructors have the opportunity to set the precedent that accessibility and inclusion are fundamental in their classroom. The following recommendations are specific to the syllabus.

- **Classroom community statement**: Include a statement in your syllabus that describes the classroom community. The following is an example statement used by Grennell in her classes. It has been included here for our readers to use as they wish, with her permission.

  In this course, each voice in the classroom has something of value to contribute. I affirm that this class is a safe space for individuals with any and all identities. I strive to make all of my classes' inclusive celebrations of diversity. Any suggestions you have on how to improve the inclusiveness of this course are encouraged and appreciated. Any concerns you have about anything related to the classroom community, inclusive practices, or anything else, I am always here to listen, reflect, and adapt.[33]

- **Accessibility statement**: To adequately capture your commitment to an accessible classroom environment we suggest providing the following pieces of information in your accessibility statement: contact information for the accessibility services center at your institution, your commitment to upholding an accessible learning environment, and the invitation to students to approach you with any questions or concerns, even if they have not gone through the accessibility services center. The following is a sample statement used by Grennell in her classes to be used by instructors as they wish, with her permission.

  I am devoted to creating a learning environment that is inclusive by design. If there are any barriers to your success, involvement, and engagement in this class, please contact me so that together, we can explore creative solutions. Individuals with disabilities may also wish to contact the Student Accessibility Services Office (insert contact information here) to discuss a range of options to removing barriers in this course, or any others, including accommodations. If you have already been granted accommodations, please contact me

Accessible and Inclusive Applications 31

so that we can work together to develop a plan that works for you and your learning style.[34]

- **Decolonizing the syllabus**: This movement has mostly been discussed in relation to ethnicity and race, but it is important to acknowledge the intersectional identities of our students by thinking about accessibility and accommodation relative to disability as well. Some institutions require their instructors to format their syllabi in a specific way or include specific language surrounding classroom policies, so we encourage you to examine institutional procedures before implementing any of the following suggestions and considerations. The main takeaways from the decolonizing the syllabus movement that lend themselves to the efforts of creating an accessible and inclusive music classroom class are:
  - **Positionality**: If comfortable, it can be helpful to identify yourself in terms of your race or ethnicity, preferred pronouns, sexuality, disability status, academic experience, sociopolitical background, cultural identity, etc.[35] Positionality is an important component of decolonizing the classroom as it asks instructors to identify ourselves and the privileges assigned to us in an effort to make our students feel encouraged and safe to share their own story and for being included because of it. However, it is important that you feel comfortable and safe in disclosing components of your identity and should not feel pressured to do so. Choosing not to disclose this information will not make your presence and experiences any less valuable. Students can still be encouraged to identify themselves with what makes them comfortable while reminding them that they are safe, welcomed, and valued in your class.
  - **Communication and access**: Provide multiple ways your students can contact you and at flexible times by hosting virtual office hours spread throughout the week, using communication features of your LMS (discussion boards, etc.), Google Hangouts or Slack, and social media. Being transparent with your students about the frequency and times you check your email/messages can help set expectations.
  - **Avoid punitive language**: When possible, avoid describing policies about plagiarism or student conduct in punitive measures. Frame these policies as an opportunity for students to learn and grow, such as offering redos for assignments or even a sliding scale approach to grades that tracks progress at various levels (i.e. beginning, emerging, or proficient). There are some institutions that require

instructors to include policies and their specific verbiage, so be sure to examine institutional policies prior to finalizing your syllabus.

- **Setting expectations**: Being upfront and clear with your students about what you expect from them both academically and socially is not only considered an action in decolonizing the syllabus, it is also one of the checkpoints included in the Engagement principle of UDL, and when addressed, promotes accessibility and inclusivity. Consider dedicating a section in your syllabus that clearly sets expectations around behavior, email etiquette, and academic integrity. Setting clear expectations can also help to unveil the hidden curriculum, which refers to the unwritten and unofficial expectations of student perspectives, behaviors, and actions acquired over the course of their schooling.[36]
- **Fostering a sense of belonging**: Empowering your students by validating their identities and unique perspectives through engagement and inclusivity is critical for generating a sense of belonging for Black, Indigenous, and People of Color (BIPOC) students. Take the time to learn your students' names, their preferred pronouns, and anything else about them that they care to communicate as one of their core values.
- **Format as a PDF**: Once you have run the accessibility checker in Word (or whichever word processing tool you are using), convert the document to a PDF for greater accessibility. Be sure to also run the accessibility checker in Adobe Acrobat before sharing the syllabus with students.

Using your Learning Management System (LMS): Regardless of the classroom modality (i.e. online, hybrid, face-to-face), it is considered best practice to share all course content and material with your students. This can include any lectures, notes, or information they might need to complete an assignment, as well as the syllabus, guidelines, rubrics, etc., used in class. Use your LMS to share content and materials with students and provide a centralized location for communications and information about your course.

- **Course organization**: Organize content in folders specific to individual weeks, or depending on the structure of the course, either by topic or section. For music examples, create separate content folders.
- **Important campus information**: Include a content folder that houses links to the accessibility center on your campus, student services, health center, campus police, the counseling center, etc.
- **Virtual office hours**: Offering virtual office hours either in addition to office hours on campus or as the sole option for office hours (especially for instructors who only teach online) opens up another way for

students to communicate with you. Many LMS's offer a video platform for use, or you can set up a free Zoom account (or any other free video platform of your choosing) and create recurring office hours on a weekly basis.

Classroom requests: If you have a say in selecting your classroom, consider the following questions when making your request:

- Is the classroom in a centrally located space that has accessible entry points?
- Can the chairs and desks be moved around in a manner that is more inviting, open, and accessible?
- Is the classroom close to the restrooms?
- Is it equipped with the technology you will need?

If you are on campus, it may be beneficial to take a look at some of the frequently used classrooms to have a specific room in mind. We understand that many instructors do not have a say in selecting their classrooms. We also know that many campuses only meet the minimal accessibility guidelines per the ADA. If you find yourself in a classroom that is not accessible, address your complaint with your department chair. Being transparent with students about the level of accessibility of your classroom ahead of time (if it is a face-to-face or hybrid class) can help them prepare as best as they can.

Accommodations: Be open to the fact that many students may not go through the accessibility office for personal reasons and might approach you directly to discuss their concerns and needs. While you can and should encourage them to go through the accessibility office (if only to avoid having this conversation each semester with every professor and not relive the disclosure process repeatedly), if it is feasible per the requirements of your institution and fair to the rest of your students, grant them the accommodations they need. If you need help in learning more about accommodations that could help a student's individual learning needs, contact the accessibility office on campus and ask for suggestions without revealing the student's identity.[37]

On-campus resources: The majority of colleges and universities have a **Student Disability Resource Center** (often referred to as the accessibility or accommodations office) that works with individual students to ensure they have the support and resources needed to complete their coursework. Make an appointment with someone at the office to learn more about how you can provide fair and equal accommodations, what they entail, and other ways to make your classroom accessible. This can also be done by email or perusing the website if it is content-rich. An additional resource on campus is the **Center for Teaching and Learning**, which can be a wealth of useful information, particularly when it comes to forging an accessible classroom. While there may not be any resources uniquely specific to the music classroom, these centers typically provide webinars, white papers, workshops, etc., to instructors looking to improve their pedagogy.

Selecting required reading: When selecting required reading materials for your course, use the following questions and considerations to guide your choices:

- Is the language accessible? Is there *too* much academic jargon that makes the information unnecessarily difficult to comprehend?
- Is the cost prohibitive?
- Are there digital and audio versions of the readings? At the very least, a digital file (i.e. e-book) of required reading should be readily available to students as they may need to utilize a screen reader.
- Can you request additional copies through the publisher to keep in the library for students to access?
- How diverse is the body of literature you are including? Try to include authors who identify as disabled, BIPOC, or other historically marginalized groups.
- Seek out publishers that provide digital copies of their texts in addition to hard copies.
- Librarians are an excellent, if under-utilized, resource on campus. If you are looking to diversify your required reading, in both authorship and medium, consider meeting with your university librarian for further guidance.
- Place your book orders as soon as possible (*at least* six weeks before the semester begins) to allow students enough time to seek alternate formats of course content (i.e. used copies, Braille, large print, etc.).
- Open Educational Resources (OER): Publicly free and accessible educational resources, such as lesson plans and textbooks, organized by discipline. OERs allow instructors to curate, without concern over affordability or accessibility, course materials that will enhance the classroom experience. Some of the benefits of utilizing OERs in your classroom are: (1) affordability for students, (2) ease of distribution, (3) course content enhancement, and (4) adaptability: OERs are not static resources and as such, they can be adjusted or modified to suit their needs.[38] Many libraries and teaching and learning centers offer additional support and guidance on OERs.

Selecting listening samples: Let us not forget what drew us to teaching music and music history: the music itself, our passion for it, its historical context, its power and purpose, the emotions it evokes. As teachers of music, we want our students to experience all of the gifts music has to bestow on its listeners, and in order to do that, everyone needs to have access. It goes beyond providing access to music and extends into the diverse nature of music selections performed or written by marginalized musicians. Selecting high quality recordings or samples is important for the purposes of accessibility. High quality recordings typically allow for volume adjustment and the ability to pause and/or playback. All audio files should be downloadable, clearly labeled, and compatible across platforms. MP3 or MP4 files are the best.[39]

Implementation and Engagement

The suggestions and best practices listed in this section are specific to being in the classroom, either virtually or face-to-face. The topics included are classroom activities, logistical considerations for both in-person and online classes, and classroom technology.

Delivery and presentation best practices: Below you will find suggestions for making your delivery and presentation more accessible.

- Provide an agenda.
- Speak slowly and clearly.
- Provide frequent breaks during longer class sessions or those that are content/theory heavy.
- If recording your audio or video, use a script and stick to it.
- Make sure what is being displayed on a screen matches and aligns with the text (this is particularly important when recording lectures or presentations).
- Be mindful of jargon, sports metaphors, regional colloquialisms (if they need to be included, be sure to thoroughly contextualize them).
- Caption videos and provide audio transcriptions.
- Carve out additional time for questions.
- For online/hybrid classes, do not require students to turn their cameras on (if this is necessary, provide advance notice).

Classroom setup: Even if your classroom requests were granted, but especially if they were not, there are some additional considerations to keep in mind regarding the setup/layout of the class. Some of these suggestions will be applicable to either online/hybrid courses or face-to-face.

- **Chair layout**: Ensure that the desks/chairs are moved around to be more conducive to that day's activity or needs of the class.

- **Lighting**: Bright lights can become a nuisance for students trying to read the projector screen, or for those with light sensitivity. Adjust the lights accordingly, and ask the class if this is acceptable. This would also make for a great question in an accessibility survey to be administered at the beginning of the semester.
- **Classroom accessibility**: If the classroom you were assigned is not accessible, communicate this ahead of time with students via your LMS as an announcement, as an email to the entire class, or as part of the syllabus.
- **Microphone**: Using a microphone is a must for large lecture halls, but they can be useful for smaller sections as well to combat any competing noises (people talking in the classroom or hallway, shuffling, construction work, etc.). Depending on your institution, instructors can obtain microphones from any of the following offices: accessibility office, technology, media, or instructional design.
- **Computer access/internet**: Ensure online students have access to the internet and a computer/tablet (see discussion of accessibility survey earlier in chapter) to complete the course successfully. If they do not, connect with your department chair and/or Information Technology office/Education Technology office to see what resources are available.
- **Tools and programs**: Informing students of the tools or programs they will be expected to use and how to use them can potentially remove learning barriers. If you are teaching an online or hybrid class, for example, and intend to use breakout rooms in Microsoft Teams, Zoom, or other video meeting platform, create an instructional guide to be shared with your students.

Listening: technology and approaches: Regardless of class modality, technology plays a pivotal role in content delivery. These suggestions and best practices are specific to the technology most commonly used in music classes (and those of other disciplines) and considerations for how to play music in an accessible and inclusive manner.

- **Provide sheet music, musical notation, and lyrics** (if appropriate) for selected samples. If meeting face-to-face, bring copies and/or have the links projected on the screen. There may be non-majors who cannot read music or contextualize films or popular music as part of the music curriculum. In this case, provide the historical context behind the selected music examples.
- **Embedding music in PPT slides**: Provide verbal instructions to your students on how they can access the recording within a PPT slide. You can also make a short instructional video of this for your students.

Accessible and Inclusive Applications 37

- **Accessible Music Technology (AMT)**: While tangentially related to this text, the growing field of AMT provides software and assistive technology for musicians that might be helpful for music students. This can include music notation software, such as Figurenotes or Golden Chord, musical instrument digital interface (MIDI), voice-activated software, multitrack recording, auto-tune, and many others.
- **Allow recordings**: Allow students to record lectures or class sessions.
- **Noise-canceling headphones**: Noise-canceling headphones can be helpful for students that need or prefer to block out all competing sounds to focus more carefully on the music being played. Some departments and offices on campus (i.e. library, accessibility services, student services, advising) might have noise-canceling headphones you can borrow for individual classes, or for the entire semester (depending on loaning policies). If borrowing from another department or office on campus is not an option, approach your chair to see if this is something that could be budgeted and then shared with other instructors in your department.
- **Share music ahead of time**: Prior to each class session, provide all music (including transcripts, lyrics, closed captions, etc.) that will be played. Make sure music examples are downloadable, labeled clearly, and preferably formatted as either MP3 or MP4 files.
- **Active listening**: Assigning tasks to students while they listen to music in class promotes active listening and increases retention. Share the tasks with students ahead of time, provide written and spoken instructions on how to complete the required tasks, and allow time afterward for reflection and discussion, if time permits.[40]
- **Structural listening**: Provide a handout that acts as a visual aid while listening to music. Study guides are also helpful (for each lesson, includes key terms, space for notes, etc.). Leave space for your students to diagram what they hear. Play music with specific structure (i.e. 12-bar blues, strophic vernacular, music or hymns, or even sonata form) and ask students to identify the structure of the example and describe their reasoning.[41]
- **Sensory support**: Sensory Processing Disorder (SPD) is a "condition in which the brain has trouble receiving and responding to information that comes in through the senses"[42] and can be seen through oversensitivity to light, sound, touch, taste, smell, etc. Students with SPD or SPD symptoms require unique ways to increase their vestibular input, allowing them to manage their senses. While it may seem counterintuitive to suggest incorporating additional tools, they can be critical in creating a reduced sensory environment for students. In the music classroom, this could be providing sensory balls or rubber bands (to be used under the foot in conjunction with the beat of the music) to

enhance the listening experience for your students.[43] Connect with your department chair or the media, technology, and accessibility offices to see if any of these items are available to use or if they can be added into the budget for purchase. If there are no budget funds available and you have the capacity to purchase some, consider buying them in bulk online to reduce the cost.

- **Movement**: Some students need to feel the music in order to authentically experience it. Regardless of whether this pull to move is due to an impairment or personal preference, encourage your students to get up and move around during listening activities if they find it helpful.

Classroom activities: Research tells us that providing a variety of classroom activities benefits all students, not only those who identify as having an impairment (s). Adding meaningful variety can help meet the diverse learning styles of students and potentially avoid classroom fatigue while also aligning with the guidelines of UDL. We do suggest creating learning outcomes for *each* exercise so that students know what they can expect to learn from the activity. Share these learning outcomes with your students before the activity begins and time permitting have students reflect on whether those outcomes were met, the effectiveness of the activity, and any other feedback they would like to contribute. In addition to the more traditional classroom activities, such as group discussions or attending a campus event or concert, below are some alternative suggestions for activities.

- **Guest lecture/performance**: Consider inviting diverse voices to expand students' exposure to different voices, ideas, topics, etc. This could be other instructors at your institution, local artists, or any friends/family/acquaintances.
- **Viewing a film**: Showing a film in class can provide an opportunity for students to think critically about the accuracy of the film's content and thematic representation. Films such as *Ray*, *Respect*, *Cadillac Records*, *Amadeus*, *Get on Up*, *DeLovely*, or *Walk the Line* can be played while students fill out a worksheet. During or after the viewing asking students to draw connections to content covered in class.
- **Listening to a podcast/speech/performance/interview together**: Select a podcast, recorded speech, performance, or interview of a famous artist or scholar that relates to the themes of your class. Provide a transcript ahead of time and notify students of the activity in case they need any additional accommodations to listen.
- **Games**: Resurrect *Rock & Roll Jeopardy!* by bringing it to your class! *Name that Tune* is also a fun way to exercise critical listening skills.

There are free and editable online PPT templates for *Rock & Roll Jeopardy!* available online.
- **Karaoke**: There are wireless karaoke microphones available as well as several free apps that can be used on your phone (i.e. Karaoke or Yokee). Give your students some notice so that they can begin thinking about their song choices ahead of time. For those students that may be uncomfortable participating in such an activity, let them know this is also OK and will not impact their grade.
- **Playing music at the beginning of class**: Make it relevant to that day's topic, provide historical context, artist or composer name, genre, etc. You could also include this in a PPT for an online class (i.e. play "A Change is Gonna Come" by Sam Cooke when discussing the Civil Rights Movement in an American Music History class).
- **Performance**: This can be instructor-led or student-led (or both!), but offering students the option to perform a piece for the class or with you serves as an excellent active learning/experiential learning opportunity.

Follow-Up Activities and Resources

Teaching and reaching our students does not end when the class is over, think of it more like a revolving door. This concise section will provide activities and resources to be used after class (either at the end of a class session, week, or semester) that can help enhance content retention and your commitment to an accessible and inclusive classroom. It is also important that our students leave our classes with knowledge, skills, and experiences they can take with them in their careers, knowing that transferable skills such as critical thinking and musical communication are essential for music educators and practitioners. The follow-up activities and resources discussed are presented with the intention of reinforcing class content, key themes and theories, and supporting students in their continuation of skill development while simultaneously reinforcing a UDL framework. However, this list is not exhaustive, and if the conversation of accessibility and inclusivity in the music history classroom continues as we hope it will, this list will grow in both volume and scope.

- **Content recap**: Provide a recap of the content covered during a specific class reinforcing the main takeaways from the content and what the students should focus on. There are a few ways to do this, depending on your preference.
    - LMS announcement
    - Static resource (i.e. PDF or Word document)

- Video to be shared on your LMS
- PPT slide included in your lecture
- Ask the students to provide the main takeaways from that day's content
- Have students sign up for class sessions and/or weeks in which they will individually provide a recap of the content OR have them guide the class in reviewing the content together
- **Additional materials**: Provide more materials on the topic should a student be interested. This could be by way of music samples, reading suggestions, podcasts, films, etc. Be sure to provide alternative formats of any additional material you provide to ensure accessibility.
- **Exam review**: From a more practical standpoint, conducting one or more exam reviews for your students can create more confidence in the material and their retention of it, leading to a less-stressful testing environment. An exam review could be instructor-led (perhaps format as a round of *Jeopardy!*) or student-led where they come to class prepared with potential short-answer or essay questions to be included.[44]
- **Extra credit**: For students who may not perform as well on traditional assignments, consider allowing extra credit as an accessible opportunity open to all students. See the Selecting Assignments section earlier in this chapter for possible extra credit assignments.
- **Course evaluations**: Find out if the course evaluations tool your institution utilizes allows instructors the option of adding their own custom questions. If this option is available, you can add custom questions that address accessibility and inclusivity as it pertains to your class. If this is not an option, consider sending out your own supplementary course evaluation where you can include your own unique questions.

Conclusion

With this chapter, our aim was to provide practical applications and suggestions for your music classroom that are accessible and inclusive by nature. Even with our attempt at brevity, it is understandable to be overwhelmed by the sheer volume of recommendations. Naturally, you will each have your own priorities as to which suggestions to begin implementing at first, but we suggest starting first and foremost with ensuring your content is accessible. This might make for more work upfront, but eventually you will learn to build these practices into your content creation from the beginning.

By contextualizing creating an inclusive and accessible music classroom as an ongoing practice, we leave room for the eventuality that new developments, suggestions, and guidelines will emerge, propelling us forward in the direction of a pedagogical approach based on the principles of UDL.

Notes

1. The suggestions included throughout this book can be applicable to the vast majority of class sizes and structures; however, there will be some suggestions more conducive to smaller class sizes and vice versa.
2. "The UDL Guidelines," CAST, accessed January 29, 2022, https://udlguidelines.cast.org/.
3. Shelley Moore, "Transforming Inclusive Education," SSHRC-CRSH, 2016, YouTube video, 3:08, https://www.youtube.com/watch?v=RYtUlU8MjlY.
4. "Universal Design for Learning," American Speech-Language-Hearing Association, accessed July 3, 2020, https://www.asha.org/SLP/schools/Universal-Design-for-Learning/.
5. To view the Guidelines, visit https://udlguidelines.cast.org/.
6. "What is UDL?" Novak Educational Consulting, accessed November 8, 2021, https://www.youtube.com/watch?v=eYN-qrKIIYI&t=113s.
7. Ibid.
8. This is not to say that an instructor should not do this, if necessary, but that UDL is intentionally designed to be implemented from the very beginning of course design.
9. This part can be rather labor intensive, and realistically, not all instructors have the resources or means to do this. Identify the degree of support and resources your department can provide when designing your course.
10. Jay Dolmage, "Universal Design: Places to Start," *Disability Studies Quarterly* 35, no. 2 (2015), https://dsq-sds.org/article/view/4632/3946.
11. Dolmage, "Universal Design: Places to Start."
12. "Web Content Accessibility Guidelines (WCAG) 2 Overview," W3C Web Accessibility Initiative, accessed November 1, 2021, https://www.w3.org/WAI/standards-guidelines/wcag/.
13. "What is Section 508?" United States Environmental Protection Agency, accessed November 2, 2021, https://www.epa.gov/accessibility/what-section-508#:~:text=Reasonable%20Accommodation,-Section%20508%20and&text=Section%20508%20requires%20that%20the,work%20for%20the%20federal%20government.
14. As of March 26, 2022, the WCAG have yet to be legally required per Section 508. However, they are considered the standard guidelines for digital accessibility. As the field of digital accessibility evolves, the WCAG are intended to evolve and be revised.
15. As defined in Chapter 1 of this book, Section 508 of the Rehabilitation Act requires federal agencies to develop, procure, maintain, and use information and communications technology (ICT) that is accessible to people with disabilities – regardless of whether or not they work for the federal government.
16. "The UDL Guidelines."
17. To learn more about the WCAG, please visit the Web Accessibility Initiative website at w3.org/WAI/standards-guidelines/wcag/. Additionally, the Wuhcag website, https://www.wuhcag.com/, is helpful in breaking down and understanding

42 *Accessible and Inclusive Applications*

the WCAG. It is important to note that these compliance levels could change in the future as the WCAG are updated, but as of April 12, 2022, these levels are still used.
18 There are many other accessibility checkers available, both free and at a cost. The W3C provides a thorough list of accessibility tools and programs. Additionally, they also provide a guide to help you select which tool(s) are right for you. See https://www.w3.org/WAI/ER/tools/.
19 To learn more, visit https://www.blackboard.com/teaching-learning/accessibility-universal-design/blackboard-ally-lms?utm_source=google&utm_medium=cpc&utm_campaign=NA_-_Higher_Ed_-_Accessibility_-_LeadGen_-_BOF_-_Search&utm_term=blackboard%20ally&gclid=CjwKCAjwo8-SBhAlEiwAopc9W3uoXM2JfTP6BknpI3MQ00z-ntzzU4J_7hZ0vHW3sWjpfbQSbUGeVBoCUxIQAvD_BwE. In the interest of transparency, Katie Grennell is currently (as of April 2022) employed by Anthology, which owns both Blackboard and Ally. She will not benefit in any way, shape, or form by mentioning this product.
20 See the following for more guidance: https://support.microsoft.com/en-us/office/improve-accessibility-with-the-accessibility-checker-a16f6de0-2f39-4a2b-8bd8-5ad801426c7f.
21 PDF stands for Portable Document Format.
22 Many institutions offer either Acrobat Standard or Acrobat Pro DC to students and faculty/staff at no extra cost.
23 "Create and Verify PDF Accessibility (Acrobat Pro)," Adobe, accessed February 9, 2022, https://helpx.adobe.com/acrobat/using/create-verify-pdf-accessibility.html.
24 For more information on these additional features and other resources on Adobe Acrobat's accessibility commitment, please refer to https://helpx.adobe.com/acrobat/using/create-verify-pdf-accessibility.html.
25 Poet is a free tool to help in the creation of effective image descriptions for the purposes of Alt Text. Visit https://poet.diagramcenter.org/ for more information.
26 TPGI offers a free Colur Contrast Analyser. Visit https://www.tpgi.com/color-contrast-checker/ for more information.
27 "Using OCR in Adobe Acrobat Export PDF," Adobe, accessed February 9, 2022, https://helpx.adobe.com/document-cloud/help/using-ocr-exportpdf.html.
28 A learning taxonomy is a framework for different levels of learning categorized into a hierarchical structure from which educators can design their learning outcomes and corresponding assessments.
29 We would like to acknowledge the emerging scholarship regarding equitable learning and learning outcomes and present both Fink's and Bloom's taxonomies for consideration. For a full list of action verbs in Revised Bloom's Taxonomy, visit: https://cft.vanderbilt.edu/guides-sub-pages/blooms-taxonomy/. For a full list of action verbs associated with Fink's Taxonomy of Significant Learning, see https://www.buffalo.edu/catt/develop/design/learning-outcomes/finks.html#title_721543227.
30 See Elizabeth Wells chapter "Evaluation and Assessment" in *The Music History Classroom* for rubric examples specific to the music history classroom.
31 There is a wide variety of music history podcasts available. Naturally, what you select will be based on your class focus, but the following are some recommendations to start with: "Dolly Parton's America," "Cocaine & Rhinestones," "Let it Roll," "Psychedelic Psoul," "The Music History Project," "Switched on Pop," "Sticky Notes: The Classical Music Podcast," or "Sound Expertise."

Accessible and Inclusive Applications 43

32 Administering a classroom climate survey at the end of the semester can also be useful, particularly if you are teaching the same class again in the upcoming semesters.
33 This statement is taken from the syllabus of Katie Grennell. By including it here, she gives her permission to readers to use it if desired.
34 This statement is also taken from the syllabus of Katie Grennell, with the intention that readers modify it to suit their own class.
35 Hossna Sadat Ahadi and Lisa A. Guerrero, "Decolonizing Your Syllabus, an Anti-Racist Guide for Your College," Academic Senate for California Community Colleges, accessed November 12, 2021, https://www.asccc.org/content/decolonizing-your-syllabus-anti-racist-guide-your-college.
36 See Boston University's "Teaching the Hidden Curriculum: Inclusive Teaching Guides & Tips" from their Teaching Writing resources webpage, found here: https://www.bu.edu/teaching-writing/resources/teaching-the-hidden-curriculum/.
37 The disclosure process can be traumatic, stress-inducing, and potentially harmful for students. Being compassionate, open-minded, flexible, and steadfast in your commitment to UDL will help you genuinely support your students as they navigate accommodations requests, either formal or informal.
38 To search for OERs for your class, please visit https://www.oercommons.org/. Here, you can search for materials based on grade level, discipline, and material type.
39 Kimberly Francis, Meagan Troop, and Michael Accino, "Six Ways to Foster an Accessible and Inclusive Music History Classroom," *AMS Musicology Now* (2018), https://musicologynow.org/six-easy-ways-to-foster-an-accessible-and-inclusive-music-history-classroom/.
40 Melanie Lowe, "Listening in the Classroom," in *The Music History Classroom*, ed. James A. Davis (New York: Routledge, 2012), 46.
41 Ibid, 48.
42 Brenda Goodman, "Sensory Processing Disorder," accessed April 11, 2022, https://www.webmd.com/children/sensory-processing-disorder.
43 Both music therapists and occupational therapists use sensory toys and tools heavily in their approaches.
44 Depending on the strength of the questions presented by your students, consider using them on the actual exam.

References

Adobe Acrobat. "Create and Verify PDF Accessibility (Acrobat Pro)." 2021. Adobe Acrobat. Accessed October 18, 2021. https://helpx.adobe.com/acrobat/using/create-verify-pdf-accessibility.html.

———. "Using OCR in Adobe Acrobat Export PDF." 2021. Accessed November 21, 2021. https://helpx.adobe.com/document-cloud/help/using-ocr-exportpdf.html.

Ahadi, Hosanna Sadat and Luis A. Guerrero. 2020. "Decolonizing Your Syllabus: An Anti-Racist Guide for Your College." Palomar College. October 18, 2021. https://www.asccc.org/content/decolonizing-your-syllabus-anti-racist-guide-your-college.

American Speech-Language-Hearing Association. "Universal Design for Learning." Accessed July 3, 2020. https://www.asha.org/SLP/schools/Universal-Design-for-Learning/.

Boston University's Teaching Writing Form. "Teaching the Hidden Curriculum: Inclusive Teaching Guides & Tips." Accessed April 1, 2022. https://www.bu.edu/teaching-writing/resources/teaching-the-hidden-curriculum/.

CAST. "The UDL Guidelines." 2018. Accessed October 8, 2021. http://udlguidelines.cast.org/.

Dolmage, Jay. "Universal Design: Places to Start." *Disability Studies Quarterly* 35, no. 2 (2015). Accessed November 18, 2921. https://dsq-sds.org/article/view/4632/3946.

Francis, Kimberly, Meagan Troop, and Michael Accino. "Six Easy Ways to Foster an Accessible and Inclusive Music History Classroom." 2018. *American Musicology NOW*. Accessed October 18, 2021. https://musicologynow.org/six-easy-ways-to-foster-an-accessible-and-inclusive-music-history-classroom/.

Goodman, Brenda. "Sensory Processing Disorder." 2021. *WebMD*. Accessed April 11, 2022. https://www.webmd.com/children/sensory-processing-disorder.

Lowe, Melanie. "Listening in the Classroom." In *The Music History Classroom*, edited by James A. Davis, 46. London and New York: Routledge, 2012.

Microsoft. "Improve Accessibility with the Accessibility Checker." Accessed March 1, 2022. https://support.microsoft.com/en-us/office/improve-accessibility-with-the-accessibility-checker-a16f6de0-2f39-4a2b-8bd8-5ad801426c7f.

Moore, Shelley. *One without the Other: Stories of Unity through Diversity and Inclusion*. Winnipeg, MB: Portage & Main Press, 2016.

———. "Transforming Inclusive Education." SSHRC-CRSH. YouTube video, 3:08, https://www.youtube.com/watch?v=RYtUlU8MjlY.

Novak Educational Consulting. "What is UDL?" 2021. Accessed November 8, 2021. https://www.youtube.com/watch?v=eYN-qrKIIYI&t=113s.

United States Environmental Protection Agency. "What is Section 508?" 2020. Accessed November 1, 2021. https://www.epa.gov/accessibility/what-section-508.

University at Buffalo Office of Curriculum, Assessment and Teaching Transformation. "Fink's Significant Learning Outcomes." Accessed April 11, 2022. https://www.buffalo.edu/catt/develop/design/learning-outcomes/finks.html#title_721543227.

Vanderbilt University Center for Teaching. "Bloom's Taxonomy." Accessed April 11, 2022. https://cft.vanderbilt.edu/guides-sub-pages/blooms-taxonomy/.

W3C Web Accessibility Initiative. "WCAG 2.1 at a Glance." 2018. Accessed October 11, 2021. https://www.w3.org/WAI/standards-guidelines/wcag/glance/.

———. "Web Accessibility Evaluation Tools List." Accessed March 16, 2022. https://www.w3.org/WAI/ER/tools/.

———. "Web Content Accessibility Guidelines (WCAG) Overview." 2021. Accessed November 5, 2021. https://www.w3.org/WAI/standards-guidelines/wcag/#intro.

Wells, Elizabeth. "Evaluation and Assessment." In *The Music History Classroom*, edited by James Davis, 103–124. New York: Routledge, 2012.

3 Case Studies of Disabled Composers and Musicians in the Western Art Music Canon

As Kenzaburō Ōe suggests, "We cannot know a culture until we ask its disabled citizens to assess it."[1] In many ways, the study of music history (or perhaps more accurately labeled, histories) is an exploration of the sonic and expressive embodiment of cultural values. History is composed of a myriad of intersecting and competing narratives, some of which are recorded while others are silenced and forgotten. Though silence is often dismissed as a form of absence, from a musical and cultural perspective, such silences are highly illuminating. As musicians, we are particularly attuned to the interrelationship between sound and silence, often finding the absence of sound just as instructive as that which is sounded. Similarly, cultural silences reveal the censorship of individuals and communities whose contribution to the production of culture has gone unrecognized. This silencing of cultural actors is evident within the study of music history relative to Western Art Music (WAM) through the historical narrative that privileges white, straight, able-bodied Euro-American men to the exclusion of women, Black, Indigenous, and People of Color (BIPOC), queer, and disabled musicians. But just as the act of silencing signals an attempt to exert power, an exploration of silences can serve to unsettle established power hierarchies and center the narratives of those who have been hushed at the margins.

The New Musicology of the 1990s made in-roads to overturning these silences by augmenting traditional methods of analysis with new epistemological lenses,[2] such as women and gender studies,[3] queer theory,[4] critical race theory,[5] and postcolonial studies.[6] This interdisciplinary approach highlighted the fact that many voices have been excluded from the WAM canon, namely those of composers and musicians from marginalized identity categories relative to gender, race, ethnicity, and sexuality. However, notably absent from this list is disability studies and the disabled experience in music, which has only been included within the past decade.[7] The addition of disability and Deaf studies scholarship has increased awareness around discrimination and the lack of diversity within classical music writ

DOI: 10.4324/9781003222224-4

large. However, there is still much work to be done, as evidenced by the continued efforts to combat systemic racism, sexism, and ableism within music. Though studies of music history in higher education have expanded to include non-Western European traditions and popular music, many institutions are still bound by accreditation requirements that necessitate a heavy focus on the Art Music canon. As such, this chapter seeks to continue efforts to expand representation within this canon by focusing on the experiences of disabled composers and performers.

This chapter is broadly divided into time periods that serve to organize studies of WAM history within the academy: the Middle Ages, Renaissance, Baroque, Classical, and Romantic eras, as well as the Twentieth century. Each subsection begins by providing historical and cultural context through an exploration of the dominant zeitgeist and institutions of the time followed by two to three case studies of composers and artists with disabilities. These case studies are a mixture of historical and ethnographic profiles of disabled composers and hermeneutical examples of artistic representations of disability that further contextualize how various forms of impairment were perceived in each time period or genre.[8]

It is important to note that these case studies are by no means exhaustive or fully representative of the works of disabled composers. Rather than tokenizing the experiences of these musicians, these case studies are meant to provide a series of snapshots of disability and music throughout time. Perhaps most importantly, these examples are situated within their historical, cultural, and political environments. This provides instructors and students with invaluable cultural context for unpacking the history of disability in the WAM canon and exploring how perceptions of disability have changed over time. Moreover, this section is designed to supply learners with the tools to challenge exclusive narratives of what constitutes music by using a disability lens to reframe music as a multisensory and embodied experience. In addition to providing a bibliography for all works referenced, each subsection also includes a list of sources entitled "Additional Reading/Listening for Students." This equips instructors with recommendations for readings and videos that are accessible to students.

The Middle Ages (400–1400)

Zeitgeist and Institutions: Disability as Punishment or Divine Inspiration?

How was disability perceived during the Middle Ages and how did this affect musicians? It is important to note that the word "disability" did not exist during the Middle Ages. Instead, impairments were described through a series of terms, including "cripple," "deaf," "mute," and "blind."[9] Much like women and people from the peasant classes, there is little documentation written from the perspective of people with disabilities from this time period. However, by examining governing social institutions and medieval law we can learn a great deal about how disability was perceived.[10] Three models of disability existed during the Middle Ages: (1) disability as an act of punishment; (2) disability as a sign of divine inspiration (Straus 2011); and (3) the religious model of disability.[11] All of these were closely tied to the teachings and attitudes of the Catholic Church, which was perhaps the most powerful institution in Western Europe during the medieval era and beyond.

The religious model of disability was primarily informed by scriptural passages from the New Testament. According to medieval historian Edward Wheatley, in many ways this model served as a precursor for the medical model of disability in that "medieval Christianity often constructed disability as a spiritually pathological site of absence of the divine, where 'the works of God [could] be made manifest.'"[12] In other words, impairment was seen as a moral flaw to which faith in Christ served as the spiritual, and, in some cases, physical cure. Such stories of Jesus healing the blind, lame, mute, and crippled are found throughout the New Testament.[13] These tales of impairment corrected through faith provided proof of Jesus' holiness and, at times, implied that disability was a result of sin, thus stigmatizing those with disabilities as morally corrupt. Though partially responsible for shaping societal perceptions of disability as stigma, the Catholic Church also provided services to those with impairments. This was primarily accomplished through the practice of almsgiving, which helped support people with disabilities who were unable to find other sources of income. Furthermore, as will be discussed in our case studies, the Church also provided patronage to disabled artists and musicians.

Many people in the Middle Ages were born with disabilities and even more acquired them through working, illness, or old age. Interestingly, the perception of an individual and their disability shifted depending upon the impairment in question and how it was acquired. While people with impairments who engaged in the practice of begging were increasingly stigmatized in later medieval society, musicians and artists with disabilities were often portrayed as being touched by God. Such double standards not only demonstrate the effect of class and profession on understandings of disability, but also point to the importance of patronage by reigning institutions, such as the Catholic Church.

Such contrasts are evident when examining the lives and works of Hildegard von Bingen and Francesco Landini, both of whom had disabilities and were praised for their genius. The significance of these musicians to medieval musical culture is demonstrated through their many works and through historical accounts from their contemporaries. Their works not only supply scholars with representative examples of musical style from this period, but also provide important clues as to how impairment in musicians and artists was conceived, depicted, and negotiated in medieval Western Europe.

Case Studies: Hildegard von Bingen and Francesco Landini

One person whose life highlights the confluence of disability, gender, and religion during the medieval period is **Hildegarde von Bingen (1098–1179)**. Though later regarded as a visionary religious leader and prophetess, her early life was marked by isolation. She was born in Bermersheim, Germany, to a large family in which she was the tenth child. At the age of three, she began having visions accompanied by "so great a brightness" that her "soul trembled."[14] As these visions continued and Hildegard predicted events which came to pass, her parents determined that she was suited for religious life and gave her to the church. Hildegard went to live in an enclosure, a small sealed room within a monastery, with another holy woman named Jutta of Sponheim.[15] Though isolated from the outside world, unlike most women of the time, Hildegard was educated and spent her days reading and studying scripture. Word of Jutta and Hildegard attracted other women and soon their numbers grew large enough to form a convent. Hildegard joined the Benedictine Order in 1113 and became abbess of the convent in 1136.

In 1141, Hildegard received a series of visions accompanied by what she described as a divine command to share her knowledge with others. She became severely ill and found that her sickness only abated after writing down her revelations. It was during this time that she began writing theological, mystical, political, medicinal, and musical texts. She recorded her visions in what is perhaps her most famous text, *Scivias* (*Know the Ways of the Lord*). The book took ten years to complete and was divided into three parts: (1) The creation of the world and humankind's fall from grace; (2) the redemption of humankind; and (3) salvation and the impending end of the world.[16] Though it was uncommon for women to be educated in this time, let alone write and share their works, Hildegard's text was read and endorsed by Pope Eugenius III, who encouraged her to record all of her future visions. During her lifetime, she earned a reputation as a mystic visionary and was widely respected as a religious and intellectual leader. This text also contained music, including a morality play called *Ordo virtutum* (*Order of the Virtues*). This play is the most famous musical vision she received during her life and tells the story of the Virtues, such as Hope, Chastity, Obedience, and Faith, battling

Case Studies in the WAM Canon 49

the Devil for a human soul. The play was intended to be performed by the nuns in her convent who sing plainchant set to both syllabic and melismatic melodic lines. Interestingly, the only role that is played by a man is the Devil, who speaks rather than sings, indicating the connection between music and the Divine. This monophonic texture demonstrates Hildegarde's adherence to the musical conventions of the time while the contrast between the spoken male role and sung female roles reveals her innovation in creating liturgical entertainment that centered the voices of her fellow nuns.

But to what can Hildegard's visions and music be attributed and how does this relate to disability? Many scholars have retrospectively attempted to diagnose Hildegard. For a time, several influential scholars and scientists, including Charles Singer and Oliver Sacks, posited that Hildegard's visions were brought about by migraines, as evidenced by both her illness and the perceived presence of aura evident in the illustrations of *Scivias*.[17] Other scholars have posited that Hildegard may have been autistic.[18] The topic of Hildegard's diagnosis is still hotly debated among scholars today.[19] However, her exact diagnosis is perhaps less important than that which her experience of difference tells us about perceptions of certain kinds of disability. Though often seen as a mark of divine punishment, due to the nature of Hildegard's visions, her disability was lauded as a sign of God's favor that provided her insight into the mysteries of the universe. Her position as an abbess not only afforded her the education and medium to express her visions, but also the protection and respect of the most powerful institution of the day – the Catholic church. Had Hildegard's visions not been spiritual in nature, she likely would not have been met with the same endorsement and may have even experienced violence. In this way, it is important to remember that Hildegard was an exceptional figure in that she was a widely respected disabled woman in a society where both women as well as people with disabilities were often marginalized. This trope of musical exceptionalism as it relates to disability is not exclusive to Hildegard but can also be observed in the careers of blind and visually impaired composers in the latter Middle Ages and throughout history.

Francesco Landini (c. 1325–1397) became blind at a young age as a result of smallpox, yet continued to be educated in the liberal arts, including the study of music, rhetoric, philosophy, and astrology.[20] He became a composer, organist, poet, singer, and instrument maker who greatly affected and contributed to the musical style of the Italian Trecento (1300s). Interestingly, Landini's chosen profession was not unusual during this time. As stated by Leonard Ellinwood in his book *The Works of Francesco Landini*,

> This affliction, which was not uncommon among musicians of the pre-classical periods, furthered his career if anything, for men continually

marveled at the prodigious memory, which he developed and at his great skill in improvisation, necessary accomplishments for a blind musician.[21]

Such assertions that Landini's blindness was actually an asset to his musical career are reinforced by several accounts by his contemporaries, who suggest that his divinely inspired musical output was a direct result of his lack of physical sight.

Though little is known about Landini's early career, scholars have significant historical evidence that suggests that he spent the majority of his career in Florence. Today he is considered one of the most important composers of the *ars nova* and is distinguished for his prolific musical output. He is responsible for composing over a third of the existing Italian music from the fourteenth century. Though best known for his organ compositions and his considerable skill as a performer, Landini also composed over 154 songs, utilizing texts from other authors as well as those that he wrote himself.[22] The most significant collection of his works can be found in the *Squarcialupi Codex*,[23] which contains 145 of his 154 surviving works.[24] The majority of these are primarily secular songs that helped establish the Italian ballata as a dominant form. Landini's ballate generally featured two- or three-part polyphonic textures with dominant thirds and sixths as heard in "Non avrá má pieta" ("She will never have mercy"). Through these works he also established what became known as the "Landini cadence," a pervasive musical motive in which the tenor voice moves down a step while the upper voice descends to the lower neighbor then ascends a third.

Blindness was undoubtedly an important aspect of Landini's musical experience and his identity, yet he did not let it openly define him. This is likely due in part to the fact that he was blind from a young age, and thus adjusted his situation in order to function within a dominantly sighted society. To Landini, his lack of sight was a part of his daily life. However, to his contemporaries, Landini's blindness was considered inextricably linked to his musical talent and to his identity as a Trecento composer and musician. Indeed, contemporary accounts of Landini describe his blindness in terms of compensation, "a zero-sum game wherein the loss of vision is counteracted by the enhancement of another sensory capacity or quality."[25] In this case, Landini's aural skills were perceived as recompense for his visual impairment.

Though Landini used much of his own poetry in his song composition, these texts were rarely autobiographical and seldom mentioned blindness.[26] The lack of autobiographical material in Landini's works is offset by the number of accounts by his contemporaries, most of which mention his musical genius and blindness in the same sentence. These accounts that align musical ability closely with lack of sight reveal important conceptions about blindness that were widespread during the time. Most evident in the writings is a paradoxical mixture of wonder at Landini's talent in the face of blindness and a sense that his lack of sight was the primary contributor to his musical and artistic greatness.[27] For example, Cino Rinuccini, a Florentine gentleman, described Landini as "cieco dagli occhi, ma dell'anima illuminato" ("Blind in his eyes, but illuminated in his soul").[28] This assertion of blindness facilitating internal sight highlights some of the underlying themes of the Humanist movement that defined the Renaissance era.

As will be discussed in the following section, Humanism was an intellectual movement that elevated introspection as the human ideal and marked inner sight as a prerequisite to understanding the human condition. Landini's musical virtuosity was evidence of this idealized inner light, a perception that was only enhanced by his blindness. Landini died in Florence in 1397, right before the time period that historians largely refer to as the Renaissance. However, the fact that such Humanist rhetoric was used to describe Landini points to the fact that Renaissance ideals were already beginning to take root in Florence. Though Landini is considered a medieval composer, his reputation as a blind musical genius, synthesis of Italian and French musical styles, and contributions to the development of vertical sonorities demonstrate that he greatly affected the development of Renaissance musical practice and contributed to changing understandings of blindness and disability.

Additional Reading/Listening for Students

Campbell, Nathaniel, Beverly R. Lomer, and Xenia Sandstrom-McGuire. "Music: The Symphonia and Ordo Virtutum of Hildegard von Bingen." *International Society of Hildegard von Bingen Studies* (2014), http://www.hildegard-society.org/p/music.html.

"Disability in the Medieval Period 1050–1485." *Historic England* (2021), https://historicengland.org.uk/research/inclusive-heritage/disability-history/1050-1485/.

McRuer, Robert, David Bolt, Jonathan Hsy, Tory Vandeventer Pearman, and Joshua Eyler. *A Cultural History of Disability In the Middle Ages*, Volume 2. New York: Bloomsbury Academic, 2020.

The Renaissance (1400–1600)

Zeitgeist and Institutions: Humanism and Melancholia

The Renaissance represented both a continuation of medieval thought and a departure from these ideals through the revival of Greek culture and the

52 Case Studies in the WAM Canon

development of Humanism. In the Middle Ages intellectual thought was shaped by Aristotelian deductive reasoning. This Scholastic order influenced by rigorous logic stood in sharp contrast to the aforementioned Humanist movement, which emerged during the Renaissance. Humanism employed philology (the study of language in both oral and written forms) to study ancient texts and translate them from Greek into Latin.[29] The Greeks had written extensively about the relationship between music, the soul, and the universe and the power of music to shape human behavior. European scholars and musicians built upon these ideals through writings of their own, as can be seen in the works of Marsilio Ficino and Baldassare Castiglione, both of whom argued for the importance of solo song in connecting the human soul with the divine and establishing oneself as a gentleman or gentlelady.[30] This emphasis on music as a medium for individual expression led to an increased demand for poetry and music, which in turn led to the development of more vernacular music styles. The spread of this music and other texts was aided by the invention and growing popularity of the printing press around 1500.

Though the religious or moral model of disability remained prominent, and was generally applied to those with congenital disabilities, a new protomedical model emerged, which "often looked to supernatural and spiritual causes as well as natural ones" and then "prescribed physiological remedies" for acquired forms of impairment.[31] This led to a growing body of proto-medical treatises and books, the development of hospitals, medical subprofessionals, and pharmaceutical remedies.[32] Despite this expansion, early medical professionals still relied heavily upon the previously established humoral model of medicine, the belief that humans were composed of blood, phlegm, black bile, and yellow bile and that illness was caused by an imbalance of any of these four components. Treatments for these imbalances abounded, from botanicals to bloodletting. Interestingly, musical practices also occupied an important place in medicine and the treatment of impairment.

Drawing upon Greek ideals, early modern scholars believed that music could either heal the bodymind or cause further imbalance. According to musicologist Samantha Bassler, "Consonant, harmonious, well-tuned music promotes healthful order. Conversely, dissonant, discordant, and out-of-tune music promotes distress."[33] Such views were influenced by the writings of Boethius (477–524 AD) in his *De institutione musica*. Building upon the previous works of Greek philosophers such as Aristotle, Boethius believed that there were three kinds of music: music of the spheres, marked by a harmony between the planets and the universe; musica humana, which created equilibrium between the body and mind; and instrumental music, or audible music sounded by instruments or singing.[34] Music was an ordered art governed by a mixture of nature and mathematics. These writings greatly influenced Renaissance musical culture, providing a foundation upon which theorists and musicians established rules for creating balanced counterpoint and developed treatments for medical conditions through musical means. The connection between music as healing or pathology is evident in both the theoretical writings of Gioseffo Zarlino and the music of John Dowland.

Case Studies: Gioseffo Zarlino and John Dowland

What does music theory have to do with the way disability was understood by people of the Renaissance? As established above, Renaissance thinkers believed that music had the power to heal or inflict harm upon a listener, depending upon the nature of the sound in question. Rules for governing what sounds were considered harmonious and therefore beneficial versus those that were dissonant and potentially harmful were essential to regulating the health and wellbeing of citizens. Furthermore, these stipulations for acceptable harmonic practices also established a "norm" by which music was judged. Thus, Renaissance music theorists played an important role in constructing standards for what constituted normative, healthy sounds and policing perceived disabling musical structures.

This is evident through the writings of theorist, priest, and choirmaster **Gioseffo Zarlino (1517–1590)**. Though Zarlino wrote extensively about astronomy, he is best remembered for his music-theoretical treatise *Le istitutioni harmoniche* (1558). Here Zarlino sought to reconcile the Greek tonal system with modern Renaissance concerns of tuning and consonance. The Greek system relied upon Pythagorean harmony, in which consonances were defined as occurring at the unison, fourth, fifth, and octave. Zarlino expanded this by creating rationale for including imperfect consonances in the form of thirds and sixths.[35] He regulated this theory of consonances through rules for counterpoint, which he viewed as "an art of bringing harmony out of diversity."[36] Chief among these guidelines were rules for regulating dissonances, such as seconds, fourths, and sevenths, which he believed should be used sparingly and only when framed by consonances on either side, such as thirds and sixths.[37] In addition to creating a pleasing experience for the listener and to reconciling ancient theoretical beliefs with Renaissance musical aesthetics, Zarlino's work also provided a basis for examining music from a medical perspective.

Many treatises of the time described the therapeutic powers of music and the connection between sound and the body. For instance, Spanish theorist Bartolomeo Ramos de Pareja argued that the four authentic modes – Lydian, Mixolydian, Phrygian, and Dorian – were directly linked to bodily humors of blood, phlegm, yellow bile, and black bile. In his treatise *Musica*

Practica (1482), Pareja asserted "that the authentic modes increased the effect of the humors which they governed, while their plagal counterparts, the Hypodorian, Hypophrygian, Hypolydian, and Hypomixolydian modes, served to decrease those effects."[38] Theorists such as Zarlino and Pareja contributed to the belief that music could either create a healing effect by stabilizing the humors or contribute to illness by creating a humoral imbalance.[39]

This was perhaps most evident in the diagnosis and treatment of melancholia, a condition that professionals believed resulted from a surplus of black bile and affected the imagination. Though the causes and symptoms of melancholia varied, music was often cited as both a treatment for this condition and, in case of melancholic melodies, a contributing factor to its occurrence. Accounts describe those with melancholia as being anxious and distracted, having hallucinations or visions, and experiencing insomnia.[40] Interestingly, this diagnosis of melancholia was abundant during this time and, as a result, representations of melancholia abound in Renaissance culture and are particularly apparent in the works of Shakespeare and the music of John Dowland.

John Dowland (1563–1626) was a lutenist and composer, who popularized the lute and pioneered lute song in Elizabethan England.[41] Themes of melancholia featured prominently in Dowland's works, such as his cycle *Lachrimae, or Seaven Teares Figured in Seaven Passionate Pavans*.[42] In addition to referencing the physical and mental symptoms of melancholia, these pieces also evoked the condition musically. He accomplished this through a repeated melodic motive that featured a "descending linear fourth ending with a plangent half step."[43] This came to be known as the "tear motive" and, in addition to being used throughout the Renaissance, was later employed in the *lamento* bass line of seventeen-century opera, such as Claudio Monteverdi's *L'Orfeo* and Henry Purcell's *Dido and Aeneas*.

Opinions varied on whether melancholy music such as Dowland's could serve as a treatment for melancholia or merely inflame the condition. Earlier some scholars, such as Bernard Gordon (1270–1330), argued that melancholic sounds would only exacerbate existing melancholia and thus suggested that one should employ a musical opposite in the form of upbeat and cheery melodies to combat the condition. Later, other scholars, such as Robert Burton (1577–1640), asserted that melancholy music could produce a cathartic effect that would mitigate melancholia, and thus works such as Dowland's *Flow my tears* and *Melancholy Galliard* provided a musical balm.[44]

The pervasiveness of melancholia and the variety of opinions related to treatment not only offer us insight into Renaissance understandings of this condition, but also illuminate how understandings of melancholia shifted depending upon the gender of the "patient." Descriptions of melancholia often varied depending upon whether the person in question identified as male or female,[45] and melancholia, its manifestations, and its perception were strictly divided along gender lines. For instance, melancholia in women was understood as madness caused by a feminine excess of emotion brought about by their perceived inherent fragility. In a society in which women were primarily seen and valued as reproductive vessels, melancholia was dangerous for the health of offspring and was viewed as a contaminant to and the antithesis of masculinity. Such misogynistic genderings of disability were clearly spelled out as "melancholia in women [was] often diagnosed in terms of lack in regard to the phallus."[46] While female melancholia was classified as pathological, male melancholia was philosophically glorified as a sign of social distinction. The experience of melancholia placed men in an elite category, particularly when such melancholy was expressed through the performance of music and poetry as stipulated in Baldassare Castiglione's *Book of the Courtier* (1528). Here melancholia was associated with masculine virtue.[47] This historical example of intersectionality provides an opportunity for students to examine the interconnected nature of gender and disability as well as how musical genres such as madrigals and lute songs reflected the gendered conception of mental health conditions as being a marker of genius in men and a form of madness in women.

Additional Reading/Listening for Students

Anderson, Susan and Liam Haydon. *A Cultural History of Disability in the Renaissance*, Volume 3. New York: Bloomsbury Academic, 2020.

McAloon, Jonathan. "The Sad Boys of the Renaissance." *Artsy*, June 10, 2019. https://www.artsy.net/article/artsy-editorial-sad-boys-renaissance.

Valentino, Andrea. "The Forgotten Bard Who Shaped Pop." *BBC*, August 3, 2017. https://www.bbc.com/culture/article/20170801-the-ed-sheeran-of-16th-century-england.

The Baroque (1600–1750)

Zeitgeist and Institutions: The Doctrine of Affections and the Seconda Pratica

Though the word "Baroque" describes Western European culture from 1600–1750, this designation was applied to this period retroactively. The term "Baroque" roughly translates to "a pearl of irregular or bulbous shape" and was frequently used by eighteenth-century writers to describe the music and art of their predecessors as strange and distorted.[48] One might even argue that the Enlightenment aesthetics of the Classical era "Othered" that of the Baroque, viewing it as non-normative, unnatural, and even disabled.

But how did people of the so-called Baroque conceptualize the music of their time and what role did disability play in the cultural production of the arts?

Much like the Renaissance relative to the Middle Ages, Baroque thinkers built upon many cultural trends set forth by their predecessors. The Humanist interest in the experience of the individual and the influence of Greek culture was further developed in the Baroque as evidenced through the popularity of the Doctrine of Affections and the birth of opera. The Doctrine of Affections grew out of the Greek Doctrine of Ethos, which held that music could shape human behavior and emotion and influence ethical attitudes. During the Baroque, this focus on the power of music reached new heights, and composers increasingly wrote music with the goal of evoking particular affections, or emotions, in their listeners. Though the previously described rules of counterpoint set forth by Zarlino and his contemporaries still held sway, new theories emerged which argued that breaking the rules of counterpoint, particularly when it came to the use of dissonance, was acceptable if it allowed the composer to stir the affections of the listener. As a result, composers increasingly used dissonance in their works to evoke emotions of pain, heartbreak, rage, and lovesickness as heard in Barbara Strozzi's "Lagrime mie" and Claudio Monteverdi's "Cruda Amarilli" among many others.

However, this new trend was not without its critics. There were many musicians and theorists who criticized the use of dissonance as unnecessary, perhaps the most notable example being Giovanni Artusi's criticism of Monteverdi's madrigal "Cruda Amarilli." Monteverdi responded to Artusi's claim that he had needlessly broken the rules of counterpoint by stating that his style of composition represented an emerging *seconda pratica* (second practice) that stood in contrast to the *prima pratica* of the past. While in the *prima pratica* music dominated the verbal text, the *seconda pratica* attempted to use music to heighten the rhetorical power of the words, even if it meant breaking voice-leading rules. This emphasis on music as a vehicle for the dramatic can most clearly be seen through the birth of opera. Interestingly, opera too grew out of Humanist fascination with Greek culture, and early opera such as Jacopo Peri's *L'Euridice* and Monteverdi's *L'Orfeo* drew upon Greek tragedy as a blueprint for creating this new art form.

Case studies: George Frideric Handel and Farinelli (Castrati)

The Baroque inherited many of its understandings of and treatments for impairment from the Renaissance. The proto-medical model of disability was pervasive. Medical professionals still drew heavily upon the humoral

Case Studies in the WAM Canon   57

model while also working to find new treatments for illnesses and develop surgeries designed to remediate physical impairment. The use of the proto-medical model and new treatments is perhaps most evident when examining the life of George Frideric Handel, who was chronically ill and became blind in his later years, alongside Johann Sebastian Bach, who also experienced visual impairment later in life.[49]

George Frideric Handel (1685–1759) was a German-born composer and musician who spent the majority of his career in England. He was a prolific composer having contributed to every genre, both vocal and instrumental.[50] Though his early career was dedicated to the creation of opera, he is mostly remembered for his oratorios, namely *Messiah*, which dominated his later compositional output. Interestingly, this shift from his monumental operatic output to the development of English oratorios coincided with a change in Handel's health. Handel was known for being ill-tempered and vacillating between highly productive periods and episodes of depression coupled with overindulgence in food and wine.[51] This was coupled with the professional and financial demands of producing multiple operas season after season for which Handel served as impresario as well as composer. Though he produced popular operas that showcased his mastery of Italian operatic style such as *Giulio Cesare* (1724), this stressful lifestyle took its toll on Handel's health. In 1737, Handel reached a breaking point while serving as impresario and composer for Covent Garden. He experienced what was described as a paralytic attack (though is now thought to have been rheumatism), which resulted in the temporary paralysis of his right hand.[52]

In an attempt to speed his recovery, Handel "took the waters" at Tunbridge Wells, a spa built around a chalybeate spring.[53] Taking the waters at Tunbridge and other spas was a common treatment during the eighteenth and nineteenth centuries for everything from rheumatism to obesity to infertility. Those who attended the spa did so from June to September and not only consumed the iron-rich water multiple times each day, but also engaged in a strict regimen of diet and exercise. Handel's six-week visit to Tunbridge seemed to provide temporary relief, yet his chronic illness was marked by another episode in 1743 that, according to contemporaries, affected his speech. Handel again sought treatment, this time at Aix-la-Chapelle, and after another extended treatment seemed to return to full health. Though contemporaries speculated that Handel had experienced a series of strokes, medical professionals now believe he had chronic muscular rheumatism that resulted in brief periods of paralysis brought on by stress.

In addition to his chronic illness, Handel also developed cataracts in his later years. By 1753, Handel was completely blind yet continued to perform concertos from memory. As with his chronic illness, Handel sought proto-medical treatments for his visual impairment in the form of couching, a procedure by which a needle is used to push the lens of the eye backwards.[54] He was couched on three separate occasions without positive results. Interestingly, his third operation was performed by "Chevalier" John Taylor, the same "medical professional" who performed J.S. Bach's couching.

Both Handel and Bach became completely blind as a result of ocular surgery performed by John Taylor. Their case studies speak to the emerging, if unsuccessful and dangerous, methods of attempting to remediate impairment that was characteristic of the proto-medical model. However, it is important to note that their experiences of both acquiring a form of impairment later in life and seeking medical treatment for these disabilities has powerful resonances with present perceptions of acquired impairment. Much like during the Baroque, today the development of chronic illness and visual impairment in senior adults has not always been identified as disability, but rather is viewed as the result of debility. Yet despite the inevitability of aging, humans in both time periods have turned to medicine to combat this process. The case study of Handel not only highlights the dominance of the proto-medical in Baroque culture (and its connection to present-day perceptions), but also serves as an important reminder that disability is a central part of the human experience and that "anyone can fall into the category of disabled at any time."[55]

However, while the proto-medical model with its focus on remediating impairment represented a continuation of Renaissance thought, a new discourse surrounding musical and bodily difference created ruptures with the past. This is perhaps best captured through the voices and bodies of **castrati**, who challenged musical and bodily normativity. The medical castration of men and boys had been performed for centuries in cultures throughout the world. These men often filled a specific social role, from pagan priests in the cult of Cybele to guardians of Turkish harems in the Byzantine Empire.[56] However, castrati occupied an important position in the musical culture of seventeenth- and eighteenth-century Europe. The procedure was usually carried out between the ages of 8 and 12 before the boy entered puberty, effectively preserving the higher range and preventing their voice from dropping. This operation (in addition to years of intensive musical training) produced a singer with the vocal power of an adult male combined with the lightness and flexibility of a female voice. The castrato occupied a liminal position, often being seen as both in-between and outside of the binary gender norms of the day. This perception was furthered by the unique quality of their voices, which was often described as "angelic" and "otherworldly."

Interestingly, the impetus behind the creation and flourishing of the castrati came from the Catholic Church. The popularity of the castrato voice spread from the Papal Chapel in Rome to the kingdom of Naples and then to other parts of Italy. Interestingly, though castrati were highly valued, the church did not sanction their creation. The act of castrating a young boy was forbidden, despite the fact that the procedure became increasingly common throughout the Baroque and was often performed by local barbers.[57] In addition to filling an important role in sacred music of the time, castrati soon became champions of opera following the edict of Pope Innocent XI that prohibited women from performing on stage. Composers began writing male and female roles for castrato singers, whose non-normative bodies and unique voices fascinated the public. Notably, many of Handel's operas featured famous castrati as male leads.[58]

Perhaps the most famous castrato singer of the time was Carlo Broschi, whose stage name was **Farinelli (1705–1782)**. He was born in southern Italy where he likely received musical training from a young age. By age 15, he made his first debut and within a few years was singing the leading role of the *prima donna* in Rome and Naples.[59] In 1724, he traveled north and dazzled audiences on the stages of Venice, Milan, and Bologna. Soon his fame spread beyond Italy and he was invited to London where he performed on the operatic stage from 1734 to 1737. In spite of the renown of performers like Farinelli, castrati were not uniformly accepted within Baroque society. Rather, they occupied a tenuous position in which they were revered in some cases and reviled in others. Opinions of castrati were also culturally bound as evidenced by the fact that in Italy castrati were referred to as "virtuoso," while in France and abroad they were often viewed as "cripples."[60] This demonstrates the conflicting perceptions of castrati as being simultaneously gifted and also disabled. Historian Katherine Crawford describes this phenomenon stating, "The musicologists offer a rich abundance of analytic attention to castrati, which tends to understand castration as enabling. But castration was also disabling: castrates were denied entry into the routines of social life."[61] A primary source of this social isolation was directly tied to Baroque values that conflated masculinity with "reproductive potency."[62] In this way, their "culturally stigmatized bodily difference"[63] and inability to reproduce marked castrati as the "Other."

This highlights the cognitive dissonance surrounding the figure of the castrato singer as someone who was simultaneously thrust into the spotlight and relegated to the margins of society. Interestingly, this seeming contradiction aligns with Baroque cultural aesthetics of the "misshapen pearl" as well as the musical values of the *seconda pratica* – the body and voice of the castrato singer defied the established gender binary and transgressed social norms in the name of artistic expression and musical virtuosity. In many ways, the prominence of castrati on the operatic stage functioned as a performance of disability, which was fetishized by Baroque audiences. This example presents an opportunity for students to discuss the connections and divergences between castrati and disabled performers today, who are often viewed as objects of fascination and inspiration by non-disabled audiences.[64]

Additional Reading/Listening for Students

Skuse, Alanna. "The Instrumental Body: Castrati." In *Surgery and Selfhood in Early Modern England: Altered Bodies and Contexts of Identity*, 16–34. Cambridge: Cambridge University Press, 2021.

BBC4. "L'Arte Dei Castrati: Part 1." *YouTube Video*. 21, no. 10 (December 16, 2014). https://www.youtube.com/watch?v=zqDEU0y9BSI.

Corbiau, Gérard, dir. *Farinelli*. CA: Sony Pictures Classics, 1994. DVD.

Gabbard, Christopher D., and Susannah B. Mintz. *A Cultural History of Disability In the Long Eighteenth Century*, Volume 4. New York: Bloomsbury Academic, 2020.

The Classical Era (1750–1800)

Zeitgeist and Institutions: The Enlightenment

From a musical standpoint, the 50 years between the death of Bach and the beginning of the nineteenth century is considered a stylistic era in and of itself. However, in terms of historical disability studies, this time period marks a transition between pre-modern and modern perceptions of bodymind difference due to the emergence of Enlightenment thinking. As a cultural movement, the Enlightenment permeated all aspects of eighteenth-century life among the elite, from politics and science to literature and the arts. Though the tenets of the Enlightenment were multipronged, its emphasis on the rationality of human beings, the aesthetic importance of the "natural," and the growth of "natural philosophy" (later called science) led to important changes in the still-popular religious and proto-medical models of disability.

Though the concept of disability as a mark of divine punishment still held sway in the eighteenth century, increasingly religious authorities drew upon Christian teachings to offer acceptance of bodymind differences.[65] In some cases, impairment was even presented as "an *opportunity* for spiritual salvation," allowing one to draw closer to God through perceived suffering.[66] In this way, disability served a moralizing function. This change was reflected in the religious model of disability, which shifted from treating impairment with contempt due to its association with sin toward a more sympathetic understanding of disability as a form of human difference.

Such shifts were evident through the establishment of institutional support for the disabled in the form of workhouses, infirmaries, and schools for the deaf and blind. Despite this change, there were limits to the compassion afforded to people with disabilities, which varied based on their impairment, class, gender, and race.

The proto-medical model of disability continued to exist in tandem with the religious model and similarly underwent changes influenced by Enlightenment philosophies. Until the middle of the eighteenth century, congenital disabilities, understood as "deformities," were viewed as "products of the whims of maternal imagination or as signs of divine intervention."[67] But as the century went on, the empiricism of Baconian "new science" spurred scientific investigation and fueled scholars to explore and uncover the mysteries of the human body and remediate perceived imperfections. This was evident through the decline of the humoral understanding of medicine as professionals increasingly "sought to demystify the causes of congenital birth defects by shifting them to firmer anatomical footings."[68] In addition to scientific inquiry and rationalism, Enlightenment aesthetics valued what was considered "naturalness." This privileging of the "seeming natural order" of things is reflected in the nomenclature used to describe deviations from established bodymind norms. Though the term "disability" was not widely used at the time, other broad terms, such as "deformity," and "monstrosity" were frequently employed to describe various forms of impairment in contrast to the "natural" ideal.[69]

It is important to note that eighteenth-century standards of "naturalness" were not tied to a specific anatomical makeup, as would become the case in the nineteenth century. Rather, the "natural" was understood as both culturally bound and closely tied to expectations relative to gender and class. For instance, it was permissible that someone of the working class might have dermatological blemishes, poor posture, and rough hands, yet such characteristics would have been unacceptable among the elite classes.[70] This was particularly true for upper-class women whose gentility was measured by their adherence to both behavioral and bodymind expectations of femininity.

Unlike the surrounding eras,[71] little research has been conducted about the place of disability during the Classical period, though musicologists are currently working to expand the scholarship in this area. While there are few ethnographic case studies tied to this roughly fifty-year period, the perception and reception of disability is encoded in the music of the time. The musical style of this era reinforced Enlightenment aesthetics of the "natural," as seen through the shifting role of the castrati in eighteenth-century opera and in hermeneutical case studies of Franz Joseph Haydn's works in which representations of disability and their remediation are communicated through harmonic language.

Case Studies: The Decline of Castrati and Disability in Haydn's Instrumentals Works

As discussed in the previous section, the **Baroque castrato** voice was prized over that of the prima donna, or female soprano voice. This was particularly true in Italy, where castrati found patronage both through private and public theaters as well as through the Catholic church. However, during the eighteenth century attitudes began to shift as Baroque aesthetics that valued drama and emotion were supplanted by Enlightenment ideals that valued the "natural" and rational. According to Marianne Tråvén, "Suddenly the artistic product of the castrato voice was considered alien to nature, and stood in opposition to both the male and female voice."[72] This intellectual shift was directly reflected in the vocal music of the time, namely the operatic reform movement seen in works such as Christoph Gluck's *Orfeo ed Euridice*, which moved away from the highly ornamented vocal lines that characterized Baroque singing in favor of simpler and more refined melodies. Though castrati continued to perform into the nineteenth and early twentieth centuries, their presence and popularity declined significantly during the Classical era.

This was particularly true in France, where castrati were stigmatized as a type of "eunuch" and shrouded in mystery. Unlike in Italy where the process of castration had become fairly ubiquitous, few French medical professionals performed the procedure. As a result, the French did not fully understand the relationship between castration and hormones in the creation of the castrato body, nor did they wish to. This is not to say that the French did not enjoy the castrato voice, which was viewed as extraordinary. Yet, as Hedy Law comments in her chapter "A Cannon-Shaped Man with an Amphibian Voice: Castrato and Disability in Eighteenth-Century France," the castrato body as divorced from the voice was a source of anxiety for French audiences: "the castrato offered a concept of otherness that could not be sufficiently explained by Enlightenment theories of the body."[73] Thus, castrati were "Othered" in the age of Enlightenment as human-made deviations that defied the natural order and confounded medical understandings of the human body. Despite the stigma associated with castrati, their public performances, especially in opera, were eagerly consumed by eighteenth-century audiences.

These more obvious examples of disability through the declining role of the castrato are complemented by less overt instances of impairment in purely instrumental music. But how can absolute music be construed as disabled, particularly without any additional program to provide context? To answer this question, we must first examine eighteenth-century harmonic language and aesthetics and their expression in instrumental genres. During this time, the Baroque practice of associating certain emotions with keys and modes (the aforementioned Doctrine of Affections) was no longer in vogue. However, Classical era composers and audience members still held strong associations with major and minor keys, often prioritizing major music over that of minor tonalities. According to musicologist Floyd Grave, minor tonalities during the latter part of the eighteenth century were associated with "sorrow, tragedy, and unfulfilled longing, not to mention the uncanny, the imperiled, the enraged, the storm-thrashed, the monstrous, and the sublime."[74,75] This association was supported by theoretical writings of the time that cast major triads as naturally occurring within lower partials of the harmonic series, which stood in sharp contrast to the "unnatural" harmony of minor triads. As a result, minor tonalities were marginalized and associated with distress and disorder.[76] Many composers used these associations to great effect in their instrumental music, particularly in the emerging genres of the symphony and string quartet.

Possibly one of the most important contributors to the creation and development of these genres was **Franz Joseph Haydn (1732–1809)**. This was especially true of the string quartet, of which he wrote 68 over the course of his career.[77] Indeed, one can trace the progression of string quartets through Haydn's works from a five-movement structure in the Fürnberg quartets (mid- to late 1750s to 1770) to the established four-movement form that came to characterize the genre. It was not just the development of the genre itself, but also the musical innovations that Haydn introduced in these works that became the hallmark of his "unique" musical style. Namely, Haydn was renowned for his juxtaposition of boldly contrasting musical themes and styles, which often served to challenge ideas of musical normativity by subverting audience expectations.

This is evident in many of his later string quartets, which drew heavily upon minor tonalities. As previously mentioned, eighteenth-century theorists and composers often viewed minor keys as "imperfect" versions of their major counterpoints. In fact, major keys could often serve as a source of "correction" for minor tonalities when the two were used sequentially. Primary themes were frequently presented in major keys with secondary themes sometimes in the minor. This allowed composers to offer their audiences harmonic contrasts, while ultimately providing them with a satisfying conclusion as the primary theme supplanted the secondary. However, this was not always the case, as seen in many of Haydn's string quartets, such as the Andante o più tosto allegretto of the "Razor" quartet, Op. 55 No. 2, which begins in a minor key. This primary theme resists aesthetic assumptions of a major protagonist by presenting an F-minor subject "constricted by pain, anxiety, and impairment."[78] Haydn then offers his listeners an energetic, balanced, and whole secondary theme in F-major, which almost sounds like a balm for its non-normative harmonic double. However, in keeping with the prescribed rounded binary form, Haydn once again returns to the seemingly "afflicted" minor for the conclusion of the movement.

This example showcases one way Haydn diverged from established eighteenth-century style by incorporating instances of unusual musical language into conventional frameworks. Despite the primacy of Enlightenment aesthetics that embraced the "natural," Haydn was praised for his use of non-normative musical figures, namely his penchant for dramatic contrasts sounded through major-minor oppositions. Interestingly, it is this very innovation – innovation that could be cast as a sort of musical impairment – that distinguished Haydn as one of the more influential composers of his time and created the hallmark sound that future scholars would come to associate with the Classical era.

Such contrasting examples serve as an important reminder that perceptions of "difference" are highly contingent. While Haydn's non-normative musical works were praised for their innovation, the physical bodies and personhood of castrato singers were rejected as deviant. Here it is important to note that representations of disability in Haydn's works are a matter of analysis and interpretation that toes the line between tradition and transformation. Though such works challenged established convention, they did so within an aural framework that was familiar to eighteenth-century audiences and were thus viewed as being innovative rather than subversive. By contrast, the embodied experience of difference as presented in the castrato body fell outside of the acceptable limits of diversity and perhaps reminded European audiences of their own precarious existence. These case studies provide an opportunity for students to consider how audiences today view performances of disability and abstract musical forms of difference and how modern audiences continue to "Other" disabled performers.

Additional Reading/Listening for Students

Gabbard, Christopher D., and Susannah B. Mintz. *A Cultural History of Disability In the Long Eighteenth Century*, Volume 4. New York: Bloomsbury Academic, 2020.

Kodály Quartet. "String Quartet No. 46 in F Minor, Op. 55, No. 2, Hob. III: 61, "The Razor": I. Andante o piu tosto." *YouTube Video* (January 21, 2016). https://www.youtube.com/watch?v=ZsMbzOIIjjs.

Prest, Julia. "In Chapel, On Stage, and in the Bedroom: French Responses to the Italian Castrato." *Seventeenth-Century French Studies*, 32 no. 2 (2010): 152–164. DOI: 10.1179/026510610X12857561930796.

Romantic Era (1800–1900)

Zeitgeist and Institutions: Medical Model of Disability, Statistics, and the "Norm"

The advent of the Romantic era in the Western Art Music canon aligns with an important turning point in the conceptualization of impairment in Euro-American society. As previously discussed, ideas of human health and typicality[79] existed before this time and were constantly shifting relative to class and gender expectations. Despite the variety of models that emerged over the centuries, prior to the 1800s understandings of the human body and notions of beauty were largely governed by the "ideal," a divine body linked to the gods/God that was unattainable by humans. However, this conception of the "ideal" was supplanted by the "norm" during the advent of industrialization in the late-eighteenth and nineteenth centuries. The definition of "normal" entered the English language circa 1840 and was defined as "constituting, conforming to, not deviating or different from, the common type or standard, regular, usual."[80] This new understanding of the "norm" was brought about by changes in the sciences and mathematics, namely statistics.

Drawing upon the "law of error" created by astronomers to locate stars, the French statistician, Adolphe Quetelet (1796–1847), created the concept of l'homme moyen (the average man), a person who possessed the average of all human attributes within a specific geographic region.[81] This preference for the "average" understood as the "norm" spread to England, where early statisticians, such as Sir Francis Galton – historically identified as the founder of eugenics – and Karl Pearson, began to use the idea of the "norm" to divide the population into standard and non-standard subpopulations.[82] Soon, those who deviated from the established norm, either through body or mind difference, were viewed as deviant, undesirable, and even dangerous. This understanding of non-normative bodyminds[83] as threatening led to the creation of eugenics, a field dedicated to studying and eliminating those deemed "defective."[84]

The development of eugenics was supported by the modern medical model of disability, which views impairment as a "deficit" located within the individual that can and should be cured through medical means. This obsession with the "norm" and the remediation of so-called "defective" bodyminds is evident from the increased diagnosis, documentation, and attempted remediation of disabilities during the nineteenth century.

Institutions were established to educate disabled people and, in some cases, segregate them from the rest of the populous. New technologies developed to remediate disability when possible and, when cure was unlikely, to assist disabled people in adapting to normative society. One important innovation that is still widely used today was the invention of braille music and literary code invented by Louis Braille (1809–1852) in 1829.[85]

Unlike previous eras, where documentation of disabilities was inconsistent and mostly captured from the perspective of medical professionals, Western European composers increasingly documented their experiences of disability and sought professional medical treatment in the hopes of correcting their impairments. Additionally, the emergence of new branches of medicine, such as psychology, emerged with the purpose of studying and remediating what was called "mental illness."[86] As a result, there is no shortage of case studies of composers with disabilities, as seen from the extensive research that has been conducted about the lives and disabilities of Ludwig van Beethoven (1770–1827), Franz Schubert (1797–1828), Robert Schumann (1810–1856), Gabriel Fauré (1845–1924), Bedřich Smetana (1824–1884), and Hector Berlioz (1803–1869), to name but a few.[87] Though each of these composers differ in terms of their impairments and the subsequent reception of their works, below we will focus specifically on Ludwig van Beethoven's deafness and Robert Schumann's experience with issues of mental health.

Case studies: Ludwig van Beethoven and Robert Schumann

The works of **Ludwig van Beethoven (1770–1827)** have long occupied a place of privilege within the Western Art Music canon, being revered as masterworks. Almost two hundred years after his death, Beethoven is still a household name and even non-musicians are familiar with the opening notes of his Symphony No. 5 in C minor, Op. 67. When asked to name a composer with a disability, many people immediately jump to Beethoven,[88] citing his deafness and then marveling at the fact that he succeeded in composing many of his "masterpieces" *despite* struggling with hearing loss. Indeed, Beethoven was and often still is cast in the role of a creative genius "overcoming" his disability to create some of the greatest musical works of all time. While it is true that Beethoven experienced hearing loss and continued to compose works that were and still are cherished by audiences, it is important to unpack the language that surrounds this heroic narrative and to situate it within its sociohistorical context. Assertions that Beethoven achieved musical genius despite having a disability are heavily steeped in the rhetoric of the medical model of disability, and perhaps this is fitting, due to the fact that Beethoven's life and works coincide with the development of this model.

Interestingly, one of the first schools for the deaf was established around the same time Beethoven began to lose his hearing. Unlike today, where schools for the Deaf are strongholds for the d/Deaf[89] community that celebrate d/Deafness as a cultural and linguistic identity, in Beethoven's time these schools promoted oralism, teaching deaf people to communicate orally rather than through sign language. Medical professionals and society alike viewed deafness as a form of "deficit" to be fixed. This shaped Beethoven's own conception of his hearing loss, leading him to seek out medical and technological innovations.[90] These interventions failed, causing Beethoven to spiral into a depression, which he documented at length in his *Heiligenstadt Testament* (1802). Here he expressed his deafness as a form of personal tragedy that made him consider taking his own life, though he ultimately resolved to continue living for the sake of his music.

While this struggle with self-harm as a result of his increasing deafness is an irrefutable aspect of Beethoven's biography, it is important for us as scholars and educators to problematize how we engage with and teach this to our students. Historically, this narrative has been presented in two ways (neither of which are mutually exclusive): (1) Beethoven's thoughts of suicide was a logical response to his deafness; but (2) ultimately, he *overcame* his depression and his deafness through and for the sake of his art. Such portrayals are rooted in ableist and eugenic notions that disability and deafness constitute irreparable loss to which death is preferable, and in so doing, devalue the lives of disabled and d/Deaf people.[91] Equally violent is the notion that disabled and d/Deaf people can validate their existence by seemingly overcoming their "conditions" through leading "normal" and "productive" lives despite having a disability or being Deaf. In truth, disabled people do not overcome their disability but rather find ways to accommodate themselves.[92] This was certainly true of Beethoven, who employed various assistive technologies of the day, including an ear trumpet and a resonator for his piano, in an attempt to remediate his increasing deafness and continued to compose.[93]

Such self-accommodation coincided with what scholars now refer to as Beethoven's "middle period,"[94] during which he repudiated his deafness while writing many works associated with themes of heroism, the most popular being his "Eroica" Symphony. In the first movement, the hero is plagued by a formally and harmonically disruptive C-sharp, but eventually prevails. Though it is important to avoid biographical fallacy, many scholars have drawn parallels between the musical hero remediating the non-normative C-sharp and Beethoven overcoming his own deafness in his musical works through sheer determination. Here there is a convergence of the medical model of disability with the pre-Enlightenment view that disability can be a mark of divine inspiration.[95] Indeed, these two narratives of overcoming disability and difference as a marker of brilliance have become intrinsic to the way we as musicians and scholars conceptualize Beethoven, his deafness, and his works today.

However, it is important to understand that the reception of Beethoven and his works has shifted over time. Though his so-called "middle period" was (and still is) praised as representing creative genius, during his lifetime his "late period" works were heavily criticized as inferior. This decline in musical style has been equated with his growing hearing loss. Following his death, future scholars utilized the three-period model as a means of segregating his later works from his earlier compositions so as not to be contaminated by his deafness.[96] These views are heavily influenced by medical model thinking. However, with the advent of the social model of disability, as will be discussed in the following section, scholars have come to view Beethoven's deafness as a form of difference, rather than a "deficit," and one that allowed Beethoven to garner his title of musical genius *because* of his deafness, rather than in spite of it.[97]

Similarly, **Robert Schumann (1810–1856)** offers scholars important insight into nineteenth-century understandings of how concepts of madness were sounded musically and how these conceptions have changed over time. Prior to the Enlightenment, issues of mental health, referred to as madness, were viewed as the result of the human mind being possessed. However, by the nineteenth century, madness was understood as being "a concrete abnormality, a form of illness or disease, lodged within an individual body or mind."[98] The new understanding of madness as illness was supported by increasing diagnoses and treatments for mental health conditions through the medical model of disability. This shift is particularly evident when examining the life, works, and disability of Robert Schumann.

Varying diagnoses have been applied to the composer, including malaria, syphilis, tuberculosis, schizophrenia, bipolar disorder, and depression,[99] most of which were attributed to him by medical professionals after his death. However, while highly clinical, the posthumous studies often serve to fetishize disability.[100] Perhaps more important is the way Schumann understood his disability, which he conceptualized as a nervous condition caused by the overstimulation of his nerves. Earlier in his life he may have referred to this through the lens of madness and melancholy, particularly after an extended period of depression in 1833 brought about by the death of his brother and sister-in-law.[101] However, after returning from his wife Clara's musical tour in Russia in 1845, Schumann began using the term "illness" to describe his episodes of dizziness, auditory hallucinations, and manic productivity followed by deep depression. Despite the medical interventions that Schumann underwent in the hopes of improving his illness, such as hypnotherapy and hydrotherapy, these symptoms continued and worsened over time.[102] In 1854, he unsuccessfully attempted suicide and subsequently asked to be placed in an asylum, where he died several years later.

Interestingly, the reception of Schumann's later works carried a stigma of defect similar to that of Beethoven.[103] In fact, Clara attempted to censor her husband's later works, sensing that they had been negatively influenced by his illness and would threaten his legacy. While some critics agree that his later works reflect a creative incapacity, this perception has shifted over time. As the nineteenth century progressed, issues with mental health were increasingly viewed as marks of creative ability. This conflation of madness, music, and brilliance gave rise to the "mad genius" trope, which was fed during this period by a combination of Romantic aesthetics in literature and the arts and developments in the burgeoning field of psychology. The resulting "powerful stereotype of the troubled creative genius"[104] created what James Deaville calls the "Pantheon of Musical Madness" inhabited by male composers such as Robert Schumann, Richard Wagner, Gustav Mahler, Hugo Wolf, Niccoló Paganini, Alexander Scriabin, Gaetano Donizetti, and Franz Schubert to name but a few.[105] These composers have been placed on the "madness continuum" that supports the false binary between "sanity" and "insanity." Despite the varying labels from eccentricism to madness that have been applied to these composers, their departure from normative bodymind expectations have earned them the title of genius. This has certainly been the case for Schumann, whose "madness" was not only seen as permeating his music but imbuing it with brilliance.

Though the trope of Schumann as a "mad genius" continues to permeate discussions of his music, it is not the only paradigm. In his book, *Extraordinary Measures*, Joseph Straus presents four interpretations that have been applied to Schumann's later work. This first aligns with Clara's assessment of her husband's later work, that Robert was mad and that his "music is also mad and therefore bad."[106] The second is firmly rooted in Romantic notions of the "mad genius," while the third argues that Schumann's condition had little impact on his later music. Though this third stream of interpretation has been supported by John Daverio's musicological scholarship in the late 1990s,[107] a fourth understanding of Schumann has emerged through disability studies. This new approach championed by disability activists stands in opposition to the medical model and understanding of Schumann's condition as a form of disease. Seen through a disability studies lens, Schumann's deviation from the norm constitutes a natural form of human diversity.

We highlight these changing conceptions of Beethoven and Schumann because they demonstrate that rather than begin a fixed entity, history is shaped and re-shaped by shifting cultural conceptions of difference. Thus, when viewed through the lens of disability studies, historical music figures like Beethoven and Schumann still have much to teach us about the role of music in negotiating, contesting, and sounding identity. While during their lifetimes, the emerging medical model of disability profoundly shaped their conceptions of their disabilities and the societal reception of their works, the social model of disability that grew out of the disability rights movement in the mid-twentieth century has offered us new lenses for understanding and teaching these composers and their music. Perhaps most importantly, these readings of composers through disability studies challenges ableist values that have been encoded into the Western Art Music canon, making room for more nuanced understandings of human diversity.

Additional Reading/Listening for Students

Alsop, Marin. "Robert Schumann: Music Amid The Madness." *NPR*. June 20, 2008. https://www.npr.org/2008/06/20/91707206/robert-schumann-music-amid-the-madness.

Frank, Gabriela Lena. "I Think Beethoven Encoded Deafness in His Music." *The New York Times*. December 27, 2020. https://www.nytimes.com/2020/12/27/arts/music/beethoven-hearing-loss-deafness.html.

Huff, Joyce and Martha Stoddard Holmes. *A Cultural History of Disability in the Long Nineteenth Century*, Volume 5. New York: Bloomsbury Academic, 2020.

Twentieth Century (1900–2000)

Zeitgeist and Institutions: Musical Modernism and the Social Model of Disability

The twentieth century was a tumultuous time characterized by global warfare, economic and technological development, and the emergence of worldwide civil rights movements. These events contributed to changing understandings of disability that occurred gradually throughout the century. In the first half of the twentieth century, the medical model of disability continued to shape perceptions of bodymind difference. The medical focus on remediating the non-normative bodymind not only led to increased diagnoses of disabilities and corresponding rehabilitative practices, but also to efforts to prevent and expel disability from the population through the rise of eugenics. Though often associated with German racial hygiene utilized by the Nazi party, eugenics first emerged in Great Britain and the United States and was widely supported by scientists, medical practitioners, and the general public through legal policies.[108] Concurrent with the eugenics movement, rising global political tensions erupted, resulting in WWI

Case Studies in the WAM Canon 71

(1914–1918) and then WWII (1939–1945). The unprecedented destruction of these wars was evident in the thousands of people who had become disabled through the conflict. For the first time in centuries, disability was ubiquitous.

While medical professionals responded to this increased presence of disability by exploring new forms of rehabilitation and prosthesis, a new form of cultural and artistic expression emerged in music. The carnage and instability caused by WWI led composers to create music that radically broke with aesthetic norms and challenged the conventions of tonal harmony. This movement was known as modernism and was championed by the "revolutionary avant-garde that rejected historical models and confronted directly the overwhelming character of the new in contemporary life."[109] Musical modernism was not only a reaction to the tempestuous events of the twentieth century, but as some scholars have argued, was a sonic embodiment and enmindment of disability.[110] As will be explored in the case study section, Arnold Schoenberg and Igor Stravinsky were two composers whose music represented these aesthetics and whose experience with disability was reflected in their late works.

Though the medical model still plays a role in conceptions of disability today, its preeminence has been challenged by the social model of disability in the latter half of the twentieth century and beginning of the twenty-first century. Unlike the medical model, which locates disability within the body of an individual, the social model separates disability from impairment. An individual may have an impairment in the form of a physical, mental, or emotional divergence from the norm. However, this impairment becomes a disability when external structures, such as society and culture, exclude and marginalize an individual because of their impairment. In this case, disability is not located within the body of an individual, but rather in an unaccommodating and inaccessible environment.[111] This paradigm couches disability as an impairment to be accommodated, rather than as a social problem to be fixed.

Just as the medical model was bolstered by the carnage of two world wars, the emergence of the social model was brought about by the proliferation of Civil rights movements in the 1960s and 1970s. The disability rights community formed around issues of access and accommodation and succeeded in securing legislation addressing educational, transportation, and working rights for disabled people.[112] Throughout the latter half of the century and the beginning of the next, disability has not only been viewed through the lens of the social model, but has also been understood as an identity category similar to that of race, gender, ethnicity, and sexuality. In this way, disability was and is increasingly conceptualized as a form of difference, rather than deficit. This changing perception of disability has been reflected in all areas of society but is especially evident in the works of Evelyn Glennie.

Case studies: Arnold Schoenberg, Igor Stravinksy, and Evelyn Glennie

In many ways, the lives and careers of **Igor Stravinsky (1882–1971)** and **Arnold Schoenberg (1874–1951)** reflect the changing understandings of disability during the early twentieth century. This is evident in their transition from modernist musical aesthetics in the pre-war period to their postwar desire to establish sonic order within a chaotic world and in their own experiences of disability later in life. Here we encounter shifting musical representations of impairment first as enfreakment, then through the lens of the medical model, and finally as personal identity and experience.

Both Stravinsky and Schoenberg contributed greatly to the development of musical modernism with Stravinsky dominating the Franco-Russian stream and Schoenberg leading the so-called Second Viennese School of thought.[113] As modernists, these composers questioned the aesthetic assumptions of the past by challenging "the concept and practice of tonality, the reliance on recognizable rhythmic regularities, the dependence on traditional instruments and sonic effects and the use of extended compositional forms."[114] This is evident through some of their early twentieth-century works, as experienced in the polytonality, changing meters, and irregular rhythm of Stravinsky's ballet *The Rite of Spring* and in Schoenberg's *Pierrot Lunaire*, the latter an atonal song cycle featuring an ever-evolving variety of instruments accompanying a Sprechstimme vocal style. These works were criticized for their disregard for traditional aesthetics and, in the case of *The Rite of Spring*, evoked public criticism.[115]

Audiences not only objected to the subject matter of these works, Schoenberg's an Expressionist exploration of the macabre visions of a clown brought on by the moon and Stravinsky's a primitivist reenactment of a sacrificial rite, but also to their musical embodiment of the "non-normative" human form. This musical expression of disability as "grotesque" aligns with the popularity of "freak shows" that became a cultural staple from around 1835 to 1940. These sites featured performers with disabilities and those who were considered cultural outsiders.[116] During shows these performers were transformed into "freaks" through the process of enfreakment, during which non-normative bodyminds are transformed into exoticized "Other" through the act of public spectacle.[117] One could argue that Schoenberg and Stravinsky engaged in a form of enfreakment through their "pervasive preoccupation with common grotesque features, including disease, deformity, and disability."[118]

For many modernist composers, this pre-war trend of breaking with convention was only intensified by the carnage brought about by WWI. Interestingly, Schoenberg and Stravinsky responded by pursuing new forms of musical order in their music. For Schoenberg, this manifested itself through his development of the twelve-tone system. Rather than using traditional tonal harmony, which is organized around a single tonic, Schoenberg's twelve-tone method allowed him to compose music by which the chosen twelve tones are organized in relation to one another. This provided an infrastructure for composing atonal music. Schoenberg applied this system to composing in more traditional forms, allowing him to meld innovation with tradition, as heard in his Piano Suite, Op. 25, Third and Fourth Spring Quartets, Op. 30 and 37, and Violin Concerto, Op. 36. Similarly, Stravinsky strayed from his pre-war modernist leanings and began to develop a neoclassical style, which embraced the style, forms, and genres of the Classical era. This shift is evident through his Piano Sonata (1924), Symphony in C (1939–1940), and opera *The Rake's Progress* (1947–1951).

Though a variety of personal, political, and social factors played into these shifting styles, it is important to consider the role of disability and disability aesthetics. Disability was not as evident in the pre-war period and composers explored musical entonings of disability through melodic, harmonic, and rhythmic asymmetry and atonality. These musical enfreakments communicated a sense of disability through the lens of the grotesque and non-normative. However, post-WWI disability became an everyday reality. While medical professionals attempted to correct the ubiquity of disability through prosthesis and remediation, composers such as Schoenberg and Stravinsky mitigated concerns of disability through "musical language that guaranteed stable balance and virtually banished the possibility of lingering asymmetry."[119]

Like many of the composers discussed throughout Chapter 3, Schoenberg and Stravinsky both experienced debilitation and impairment acutely in their later years. Throughout his life, Schoenberg experienced chronic illness in the form of asthma, and later diabetes and a heart condition. In many ways, his later works reflect his deteriorating health and non-normative bodily condition. This is particularly evident in his String Trio (1946), which chronicles his near death experience after having a heart attack.[120] While this trio communicates a recovery narrative, Stravinsky's *Requiem Canticles* (1966) reflects his resigned acceptance of his disability resulting from polycythemia and a subsequent stroke.[121] Though he died before the social model of disability was widespread, Stravinsky's musical embodiment and subsequent acceptance of his disability (rather than an attempt to "cure" it) highlights a shift away from medical model thinking towards an understanding of disability as a personal and creative identity.

This embrace of disability as an identity is observable in percussionist, composer, and performer **Evelyn Glennie (b. 1965)**, who asserts that her experience with deafness has not only profoundly shaped her career but has also impacted the way she conceptualizes music. Glennie began to lose her hearing at the age of eight and by twelve was deaf. She continued to play music and percussion though her relationship with sound shifted from being centered in the auditory nerve to the entire body. Glennie has enhanced her experience of this musical embodiment by performing barefoot in order to better feel the vibration of soundwaves. After becoming deaf, Glennie continued to pursue her musical studies as a percussionist and became the first deaf person to attend the Royal Academy of Music. Since this time, she has established herself as the first person to attain international success as a full-time solo percussionist. In addition to performing with orchestras around the globe, Glennie has also produced over 40 albums, which vary from original and commissioned works to percussion concerti.

Though her career as a performer has earned her international acclaim, Glennie states that her main mission in life is to teach people how to listen. Glennie believes that "there is no such thing as silence" and has explored this topic and the process of listening through many talks she has given around the world and in her book, *Listen World!: The Life of Percussion* (2019). Glennie has drawn upon her experience as a deaf percussionist to challenge misconceptions of silence and hearing. Specifically, she encourages people to think more broadly about the nature of sound and what it means to connect with other people through the process of listening multisensorially. This notion of music and sound as extending beyond the ear is an important topic of discussion for music students who are educated in hearing-dominant institutions and provides the opportunity to consider how expanding notions of music is a form of inclusivity.

In this way, Glennie is not only a world-class performer and composer, but also a disability advocate. As will be discussed in the Dip Hop section of Chapter 4, many people in the Deaf community do not consider d/Deafness to be a disability, but rather view it as a cultural identity. Members of the Deaf community communicate through sign language, thus marking those who identify as Deaf as a linguistic and cultural identity group. However, Glennie was not raised in a culturally Deaf environment, though she has recently become more involved in the Deaf community and is learning sign language. Her embrace of deafness and engagement in sound activism reflects the changing understandings of disability and difference that began to take place in the 1960s. These shifting conceptions of disability à la the social model continue to shape disability discourse in the twenty-first century.

Additional Reading/Listening for Students

Glennie, Evelyn. "How to Truly Listen." Filmed February 2003 in Oxford, United Kingdom. TED video, https://www.ted.com/talks/evelyn_glennie_how_to_truly_listen.

Glennie, Evelyn, Sander L. Gilman, and Youn Kim. "Is There Disabled Music?: Music and the Body from Dame Evelyn Glennie's Perspective." In *The Oxford Handbook of Music and the Body*, edited by Sander L. Gilman and Youn Kim, 318–332. New York: Oxford University Press, 2015.

Mitchell, David T. and Sharon L. Snyder. *A Cultural History of Disability in the Modern Age*, Volume 6. New York: Bloomsbury Academic, 2020.

Conclusion

Though by no means exhaustive, we have endeavored to provide a digestible overview of the changing conceptions of disability in Western Art Music from the Middle Ages through the twenty-first century. Many of the composers and case studies represented in this chapter coincide with the material frequently covered in Western Music History classes and thus provide instructors with examples they can easily incorporate into their curriculum. As demonstrated through these case studies, disability is pervasive within the Western Art Music canon. However, impairment and disability are rarely discussed in textbooks that guide most music history curricula. This reveals the ways in which disability histories have been silenced within music education. In this way, these case studies not only provide instructors with the tools to counteract this erasure, but also demonstrate to students that music history is a multifaceted and rich subject that is ever evolving. Moreover, such examples allow disabled students to feel represented in the music they study and facilitate their access to and engage with the curriculum.

Notes

1 Sharon L. Snyder and David T. Mitchell, *Narrative Prosthesis: Disability and Its Dependencies of Discourse* (Ann Arbor, MI: University of Michigan Press, 2000), 178.
2 Joseph Kerman, *Contemplating Music: Challenges to Musicology* (Cambridge, MA: Harvard University Press, 1985).
3 Marcia Citron, *Gender and the Musical Canon* (New York: Cambridge University Press, 1993); Susan McClary, *Feminine Endings* (Minneapolis, MN: University of Minnesota Press, 1991); Ruth Solie, *Musicology and Difference: Gender and Sexuality in Music Scholarship* (Berkeley, CA: University of California Press, 1993).
4 Philip Brett, Elizabeth Wood, and Gary C. Thomas, eds., *Queering the Pitch: The New Gay and Lesbian Musicology* (New York: Routledge, 1994).

5 Ronald Radano and Philip Bohlman, *Music and the Racial Imagination* (Chicago, IL: The University of Chicago Press, 2000).
6 Kofi Agawu, *Representing African Music: Postcolonial Notes, Queries, Positions* (New York: Routledge, 2003).
7 Michael B. Bakan, *Speaking for Ourselves: Conversations on Life, Music, and Autism* (New York: Oxford University Press, 2018); Blake Howe, Stephanie Jensen-Moulton, Neil Lerner, and Joseph Straus, *The Oxford Handbook of Music and Disability Studies* (New York: Oxford University Press, 2015); Alex Lubet, *Music, Disability, and Society* (Philadelphia, PA: Temple University Press, 2011); Neil Lerner and Joseph Straus, *Sounding Off: Theorizing Disability in Music* (New York: Routledge, 2006); Joseph Straus, *Extraordinary Measures: Disability in Music* (New York: Oxford University Press, 2011).
8 Blake Howe, Stephanie Jensen-Moulton, Joseph N. Straus, Jennifer Iverson, Jessica A. Holmes, Michael B. Bakan, Andrew Dell'Antonio, and Elizabeth J. Grace, "On the Disability Aesthetics of Music," *Journal of the American Musicological Society* 69, no. 2 (2016): 525–563, https://doi-org.pallas2.tcl.sc.edu/10.1525/jams.2016.69.2.525.
9 Here these terms are presented in English though they would have appeared in their respective languages throughout Europe.
10 Irina Metzler, *A Social History of Disability in the Middle Ages: Cultural Considerations of Physical Impairment* (New York: Routledge, 2013).
11 Edward Wheatley, *Stumbling Blocks before the Blind: Medieval Constructions of a Disability* (Ann Arbor, MI: University of Michigan Press, 2010), 11.
12 Ibid.
13 It is important to note that while this terminology is no longer used today to describe physical impairments, these terms would have been used during the Middle Ages, and thus appear here.
14 Peter Dronke, *Women Writers of the Middle Ages* (Cambridge: Cambridge University Press, 1984), 145.
15 Susan Signe Morrison, *A Medieval Woman's Companion: Women's Lives in the European Middle Ages* (Havertown, PA: Oxbow Books, 2015), 106.
16 Jay Ruud, "Scivias," in *Encyclopedia of Medieval Literature*, 2nd edition, accessed October 25, 2021, https://login.pallas2.tcl.sc.edu/login?url=https://search.credoreference.com/content/entry/fofmedieval/scivias/0?institutionId=6481.
17 Madeline Caviness, *Art in the Medieval West and its Audience* (Aldershot: Ashgate, 2001); Sabrina Flanagan, *Hildegard of Bingen, 1098–1179: A Visionary Life* (New York: Routledge, 1989); Oliver Sacks, *Migraine: Revised and Expanded* (New York: Vintage Books, 1992); Charles Singer, *Studies in the History and Method of Science* (Oxford: Clarendon Press, 1917).
18 Patricia Ranft, "Ruminations on Hildegard of Bingen (1098–1179) and Autism," *Journal of Medical Biography* 22, no. 2 (2014): 107–115, https://doi.org/10.1177/0967772013479283.
19 For nuanced discussion of the power of retrospective diagnosis, see Katherine Foxhall, "Making Modern Migraine Medieval: Men of Science, Hildegard of Bingen, and the Life of a Retrospective Diagnosis," *Medical History* 58, no. 3 (2014): 354–374.
20 Leonard Ellinwood, *The Works of Francesco Landini* (Cambridge, MA: The Medieval Academy of America, 1945), xvi.

21 Ellinwood, *The Works of Francesco Landini*, xvi.
22 Julie Singer, "Playing by Ear: Compensation, Reclamation, and Prosthesis in Fourteenth-Century Song," in *Disability in the Middle Ages: Reconsiderations and Reverberations*, ed. Joshua R. Eyler (Burlington, VT: Ashgate Publishing Company, 2010), 43.
23 For more information about the *Squarcialupi Codex* visit the University of Miami's Music for the Eyes: Manuscripts from the Frank Cooper Music Facsimile Collection: http://scholar.library.miami.edu/facsimile/squarcialupi.html.
24 Kurt von Fischer and Gianluca D'Agostino, "Landini, Francesco," *Grove Music Online* (2001), https://doi.org/10.1093/gmo/9781561592630.article.15942.
25 Singer, "Playing by Ear," 42.
26 While his song "Ochi dolente mie" ("My pained eyes") does reference blindness, there is little evidence that this song refers to Landini's own experience.
27 This trope of sensory compensation, the belief that blind people develop heightened senses to compensate for their inability to see, is pervasive. For greater discussion see Terry Rowden, *The Songs of Blind Folk: African American Musicians and the Cultures of Blindness* (Ann Arbor, MI: University of Michigan Press, 2009) and Georgina Kleege, "Blindness and Visual Culture: An Eyewitness Account," in *The Disability Studies Reader*, 4th edition, ed. Lennard J. Davis (New York: Routledge, 2013), 447–455.
28 Singer, "Playing by Ear," 39–52.
29 Richard Freedman, *Music in the Renaissance* (New York: W.W. Norton and Company, 2013), 94.
30 Ibid, 95.
31 Allison Hobgood, *Beholding Disability in Renaissance England* (Ann Arbor, MI: University of Michigan Press, 2021), 30. There was an interest in treating congenital forms of disability. However, in general, congenital disabilities were viewed as something permanent, while people increasingly explored remedies for acquired impairments.
32 Ibid, 31.
33 Samantha Bassler, "Madness and Music as (Dis)ability in Early Modern England," in *The Oxford Handbook of Music and Disability Studies*, eds. Blake Howe, Stephanie Jensen-Moulton, Neil Lerner, and Joseph Straus (New York: Oxford University Press, 2015). DOI: 10.1093/oxfordhb/9780199331444.013.46
34 Ibid.
35 Claude V. Palisca, "Zarlino, Gioseffo," *Grove Music Online*, accessed June 8, 2021, https://doi.org/10.1093/gmo/9781561592630.article.30858.
36 Claude V. Palisca, "Baroque," *Grove Music Online*, accessed June 13, 2021, https://doi.org/10.1093/gmo/9781561592630.article.02097.
37 Freedman, *Music in the Renaissance*, 252.
38 Christopher Callahan, "Music in Medieval Medical Practice: Speculations and Certainties," *College Music Symposium*, last modified October 17, 2018, https://symposium.music.org/index.php/40/item/2168-music-in-medieval-medical-practice-speculations-and-certainties#x21.
39 For instance, John Wilbye's madrigal "Draw on, sweet Night" allows the musician to engage in a homeopathic cure through performance by sharing in the melancholy of the speaker.
40 Freedman, *Music in the Renaissance*, 103.

41 Peter Holman and Paul O'Dette, "Downland, John," *Grove Music Online*, accessed June 8, 2021, https://doi.org/10.1093/gmo/9781561592630.article.08103.
42 Freedman, *Music in the Renaissance*, 104.
43 Ibid.
44 Freedman, *Music in the Renaissance*, 105–106.
45 Bassler, "Madness and Music as (Dis)ability in Early Modern England."
46 Juliana Schiersari, *The Gendering of Melancholia* (Ithaca, NY: Cornell University Press, 1992), 96.
47 Freedman, *Music in the Renaissance*, 111.
48 Palisca, "Baroque," 2001.
49 Ahti Tarkkanen. "Blindness of Johann Sebastian Bach," *Acta Ophthalmologica* 91 (2013):191–192.
50 Anthony Hicks, "Handel [Händel, Hendel], George Frideric [Georg Friederich]," *Grove Music Online*, accessed June 13, 2021, https://doi.org/10.1093/gmo/9781561592630.article.40060.
51 Some scholars have uncovered evidence that Handel perhaps had bulimia nervosa. See David Hunter, "Handel's Ill Health: Documents and Diagnoses," *Royal Musical Association Research Chronicle*, no. 41 (2008): 80.
52 Hicks, "Handel."
53 John M. Ford, "Taking the Waters at Tunbridge Wells," *Stress Medicine* 2 (1986): 170.
54 Milo Keynes, "Handel and His Illness," *The Musical Times* 123, no. 1675 (1982): 614.
55 Elizabeth F. Emens, "Disabling Attitudes: U.S. Disability Law and the ADA Amendments Act," in *The Disability Studies Reader*, 4th edition, ed. Lennard J. Davis (New York: Routledge, 2013), 50.
56 Patrick Barbier, *The World of the Castrati: The History of an Extraordinary Operatic Phenomenon*, trans. Margaret Crosland (London: Souvenir Press, 1996), 6–7.
57 During this time barbers were not only responsible for cutting hair but also performing surgical procedures.
58 The premiere of *Guilio Cesare* featured three famous castrati: Senesino as Julius Cesare, Gaetano Berenstadt as Tolomeo, and Giuseppe Bigonzi as Nireno.
59 Ellen T. Harris, "Farinelli [Broschi, Carlo; Farinello," *Grove Music Online*, accessed June 18, 2021, https://doi.org/10.1093/gmo/9781561592630.article.09312.
60 Barbier, *The World of the Castrati*, 2.
61 Katherine Crawford, *Eunuchs and Castrati: Disability and Normativity in Early Modern Europe* (New York: Routledge, 2019), 4.
62 Ibid, 5.
63 Joseph N. Straus, *Extraordinary Measures: Disability in Music* (New York: Oxford University Press, 2011), 9.
64 Katie Ellis, *Disability and Popular Culture Focusing Passion, Creating Community and Expressing Defiance* (Farnham, Great Britain: Routledge, 2016), 102.
65 David M. Turner, *Disability in Eighteenth-Century England: Imagining Physical Impairment* (New York: Routledge, 2012), 38.
66 Ibid.
67 Ibid, 5.

68 Turner, *Disability in Eighteenth-Century England: Imagining Physical Impairment*, 57.
69 Ibid, 27–28.
70 Ibid, 29.
71 It is important to note that eras are not temporally fixed but rather are constructed by historians retroactively.
72 Marianne Tråvén, "Voicing the Third Gender: The Castrato Voice and the Stigma of Emasculation in Eighteenth-Century Society," *Études Épistémè* 29 (2016), https://doi.org/10.4000/episteme.1220.
73 Hedy Law, "A Cannon-Shaped Man with an Amphibian Voice: Castrato and Disability in Eighteenth-Century France," in *The Oxford Handbook of Music and Disability Studies*, eds. Blake Howe, Stephanie Jensen-Moulton, Neil Lerner, and Joseph Straus (New York: Oxford University Press, 2015), 11.
74 Floyd Grave, "Narratives of Affliction and Recovery in Haydn," in *The Oxford Handbook of Music and Disability Studies*, eds. Blake Howe, Stephanie Jensen-Moulton, Neil Lerner, and Joseph Straus (New York: Oxford University Press, 2015), 10.
75 This storm-like musical style, called *Sturm und Drang*, was regularly used by composers and communicated through sudden shifts in dynamics, chromaticism, and use of the minor mode.
76 Grave, "Narratives of Affliction and Recovery in Haydn," 10.
77 Georg Feder and James Webster, "Haydn, (Franz) Joseph," *Grove Music Online*, accessed June 25, 2021, https://doi.org/10.1093/gmo/9781561592630.article.44593.
78 Grave, "Narratives of Affliction and Recovery in Haydn," 7.
79 Here typicality refers to the societally established standard of bodymind composition and behavior.
80 Lennard J. Davis, "Introduction: Normality, Power, and Culture," in *The Disability Studies Reader*, 4th edition, ed. Lennard J. Davis (New York: Routledge, 2013), 1.
81 Ibid, 2.
82 Francis Galton, *Inquiries into Human Faculty* (London: Macmillan, 1883).
83 The criteria for determining who deviated from the norm was heavily imbued with value judgments about "difference" that conflated impairment with other markers of identity, such as nationality, ethnicity, race, gender, and sexuality.
84 For more information about eugenics, see Jay Timothy Dolmage, *Disabled upon Arrival: Eugenics, Immigration, and the Construction of Race and Disability* (Columbus, OH: Ohio State University Press, 2018); Douglas C. Baynton, *Defectives in the Land: Disability and Immigration in the Age of Eugenics* (Chicago, IL: University of Chicago Press, 2016).
85 Shersten Johnson, "Notational Systems and Conceptualizing Music: A Case Study of Print and Braille Notation," *Music Theory Online* 15, no. 3–4, August 2009, https://mtosmt.org/issues/mto.09.15.3/mto.09.15.3.johnson.html.
86 Today this term is rejected as narrowly aligning with the medical model of disability and promoting sanism, social stigma, and oppression against mental difference. While terminology varies widely among people who experience issues of mental health, more recently the Mad Pride Movement has reclaimed the term "mad" to describe those with mental differences.
87 This is also helped in large part by the fact that there is extensive documentation about and from the lives of these composers.

88 This is also due to the many films that have been made about his life, such as *Un Grand Amour de Beethoven* (1936), *Immortal Beloved* (1994), and *Copying Beethoven* (2006).
89 Here the lowercase "d" refers to the physical condition of deafness, while the uppercase "D" is used to express the importance of the Deaf cultural experience as separate from yet connected to the physical condition.
90 Though scholars are unable pinpoint the exact cause of Beethoven's deafness, according to Robin Wallace it was the result of sensorineural hearing loss, which "stems from malfunctions in the inner ear itself, where the sense of hearing is centered, or in the nerves that transmit its signal to the brain" (13).
91 People who are culturally Deaf do not consider deafness to be a disability, but rather a cultural and linguistic marker of identity. However, Beethoven was not culturally Deaf and did think of his deafness as a form of impairment.
92 The degree to which people are able to successfully accommodate themselves depends largely on the accessibility of their environment.
93 Robin Wallace, *Hearing Beethoven: A Story of Musical Loss and Discovery* (Chicago, IL: University of Chicago Press, 2018).
94 Though the "three period model" popularized by Lenz in 1852 dominated musicological discourse surrounding Beethoven's works for centuries, this paradigm has come under scrutiny more recently by Joseph Kerman, Alan Tyson, and Scott G. Burnham, who advocated for adding a fourth period.
95 Straus, *Extraordinary Measures*, 54.
96 Wallace argues that the critique of Beethoven's late works has less to do with their length and demands on the performer and listener, which could also be said of his celebrated middle-period works, and more to do with the fact that they were viewed through the lens of deafness (73).
97 Ibid.
98 Straus, *Extraordinary Measures*, 33.
99 Ibid, 34.
100 James Deaville, "Sounds of Mind: Music and Madness in the Popular Imagination," in *The Oxford Handbook of Music and Disability Studies*, eds. Blake Howe, Stephanie Jenson-Moulton, Neil Lerner, and Joseph Straus (New York: Oxford University Press, 2015), 640–660.
101 Ibid.
102 Straus, *Extraordinary Measures*, 36.
103 For further discussion of actual and perceived disability the late style of composers see Joseph Straus, "Disability and 'Late Style' in Music," 2008, *The CUNY Graduate Center*, accessed November 5, 2021, https://academicworks.cuny.edu/gc_pubs/417/.
104 Deaville, "Sounds of Mind," 645.
105 Ibid.
106 Straus, *Extraordinary Measures*, 37.
107 John Daverio and Eric Sams, "Schumann, Robert," *Grove Music Online*, accessed July 3, 2021, https://doi.org/10.1093/gmo/9781561592630.article.40704.
108 A number of noted persons advocated eugenics to one extent or another, such as Theodore Roosevelt and Alexander Graham Bell. These ranged from overt legislation that sanctioned sterilization of disabled people to more coded laws that restricted immigration, demonstrating the intersectional nature of disability and other minority identities. This also extended to "ugly laws," which were established in the late nineteenth century. See Susan M. Schweik and Robert A.

Wilson, "Ugly Laws," February 5, 2015, https://eugenicsarchive.ca/discover/connections/54d39e27f8a0ea47060.
109 Leon Botstein, "Modernism," *Grove Music Online*, accessed July 14, 2021, https://doi.org/10.1093/gmo/9781561592630.article.40625.
110 Joseph N. Straus, *Broken Beauty: Musical Modernism and the Representation of Disability* (New York: Oxford University Press, 2018).
111 Tom Shakespeare, "The Social Model of Disability," in *The Disability Studies Reader*, 4th edition, ed. Lennard J. Davis (New York: Routledge, 2013), 216.
112 For more information on these movements in the United States and Europe see Emens, "Disabling Attitudes"; Lukin, "Disability and Blackness"; and Shakespeare, "The Social Model of Disability."
113 Botstein, "Modernism."
114 Ibid.
115 Stephen Walsh, "Stravinsky, Igor (Fyodorovich)," *Grove Music Online*, accessed July 14, 2021, https://doi.org/10.1093/gmo/9781561592630.article.52818.
116 For further discussion of the intersectionality of gender, race, ethnicity, and disability in freak shows, see Rosemarie Garland-Thomson, *Extraordinary Bodies: Figuring Physical Disability in American Culture and Literature* (New York: Columbia University Press, 1997).
117 Garland-Thomson, *Extraordinary Bodies*, 17.
118 Straus, *Extraordinary Measures*, 77.
119 Ibid, 81.
120 For deeper analysis of this piece as it relates to Schoenberg's disability, see Straus's *Extraordinary Measures*.
121 Polycythemia is an increase in red blood cell count that increases the risk of blood clots and stroke.

References

Agawu, Kofi. *Representing African Music: Postcolonial Notes, Queries, Positions*. New York: Routledge, 2003.
Bakan, Michael B. *Speaking for Ourselves: Conversations on Life, Music, and Autism*. New York: Oxford University Press, 2018.
Barbier, Patrick. *The World of the Castrati: The History of an Extraordinary Operatic Phenomenon*. Translated by Margaret Crosland. London: Souvenir Press, 1996.
Bassler, Samantha. "Madness and Music as (Dis)ability in Early Modern England." In *The Oxford Handbook of Music and Disability Studies*, edited by Blake Howe, Stephanie Jensen-Moulton, Neil Lerner, and Joseph Straus. New York: Oxford University Press, 2015. 529–538. https://doi.org/10.1093/oxfordhb/97801993314444.013.46.
Baynton, Douglas C. *Defectives in the Land: Disability and Immigration in the Age of Eugenics*. Chicago, IL: University of Chicago Press, 2016.
Botstein, Leon. "Modernism." Grove Music Online. Accessed July 14, 2021. https://doi.org/10.1093/gmo/9781561592630.article.40625.
Brett, Philip, Elizabeth Wood, and Gary C. Thomas, eds. *Queering the Pitch: The New Gay and Lesbian Musicology*. New York: Routledge, 1994.

Callahan, Christopher. "Music in Medieval Medical Practice: Speculations and Certainties." *College Music Symposium*. Last modified October 17, 2018. https://symposium.music.org/index.php/40/item/2168-music-in-medieval-medical-practice-speculations-and-certainties#x21.

Caviness, Madeline. *Art in the Medieval West and its Audience*. Aldershot: Ashgate, 2001.

Citron, Marcia. *Gender and the Musical Canon*. New York: Cambridge University Press, 1993.

Crawford, Katherine. *Eunuchs and Castrati: Disability and Normativity in Early Modern Europe*. New York: Routledge, 2019.

Cuthbert, Michael Scott. "Difference, Disability, and Composition in the Late Middle Ages: Of Antonio "Zachara" da Teramo and Francesco "Il Cieco" da Firenze." In *The Oxford Handbook of Music and Disability Studies*, edited by Blake Howe, Stephanie Jensen-Moulton, Neil Lerner, and Joseph Straus, 517–528. New York: Oxford University Press. https://doi.org/10.1093/oxfordhb/9780199331444.013.27.

Daverio, John, and Eric Sams. "Schumann, Robert." Grove Music Online. Accessed July 3, 2021. https://doi.org/10.1093/gmo/9781561592630.article.40704.

Davis, Lennard J. "Introduction: Normality, Power, and Culture." In *The Disability Studies Reader*, 4th edition, edited by Lennard J. Davis, 1–14. New York: Routledge, 2013.

Deaville, James. "Sounds of Mind: Music and Madness in the Popular Imagination." In *The Oxford Handbook of Music and Disability Studies*, edited by Blake Howe, Stephanie Jensen-Moulton, Neil Lerner, and Joseph Straus. New York: Oxford University Press, 2015, https://doi.org/10.1093/oxfordhb/9780199331444.013.8.

Dolmage, Jay Timothy. *Disabled upon Arrival: Eugenics, Immigration, and the Construction of Race and Disability*. Columbus, OH: Ohio State University Press, 2018.

Dronke, Peter. *Women Writers of the Middle Ages*. Cambridge: Cambridge University Press, 1984.

Ellinwood, Leonard. *The Works of Francesco Landini*. Cambridge: The Medieval Academy of America, 1945.

Ellis, Katie. *Disability and Popular Culture: Focus Passion, Creating Community and Expressing Deviance*. Burlington, VT: Ashgate, 2015.

Emens, Elizabeth F. "Disabling Attitudes: U.S. Disability Law and the ADA Amendments Act." In *The Disability Studies Reader*, 4th edition, edited by Lennard J. Davis, 42–57. New York: Routledge, 2013.

Feder, Georg and James Webster. "Haydn, (Franz) Joseph." Grove Music Online. Accessed June 25, 2021. https://doi.org/10.1093/gmo/9781561592630.article.44593.

Fischer, Kurt von, and Gianluca D'Agostino. 2001. "Landini, Francesco." Grove Music Online. Accessed May 24, 2021. https://doi.org/10.1093/gmo/9781561592630.article.15942.

Flanagan, Sabrina. *Hildegard of Bingen, 1098–1179: A Visionary Life*. New York: Routledge, 1989.

Ford, John M. "Taking the Waters at Tunbridge Wells." *Stress Medicine* 2 (1986): 169–174.

Foxhall, Katherine. 2014. "Making Modern Migraine Medieval: Men of Science, Hildegard of Bingen, and the Life of a Retrospective Diagnosis." *Medical History*, 58 no. 3, 354–374. Accessed October 25, 2021. https://doi.org/10.1017/mdh.2014.28.

Freedman, Richard. *Music in the Renaissance*. New York: W.W. Norton and Company, 2013.

Galton, Francis. *Inquiries into Human Faculty*. London: Macmillan, 1883.

Garland-Thomson, Rosemarie. *Extraordinary Bodies: Figuring Physical Disability in American Culture and Literature*. New York: Columbia University Press, 1997.

Grave, Floyd. "Narratives of Affliction and Recovery in Haydn." In *The Oxford Handbook of Music and Disability Studies*, edited by Blake Howe, Stephanie Jensen-Moulton, Neil Lerner, and Joseph Straus, 563–589. New York: Oxford University Press, 2015. https://doi.org/10.1093/oxfordhb/9780199331444.013.28.

Harris, Ellen T. "Farinelli [Broschi, Carlo; Farinello." Grove Music Online. Accessed June 18, 2021. https://doi.org/10.1093/gmo/9781561592630.article.09312.

Hicks, Anthony. "Handel [Händel, Hendel], George Frideric [Georg Friederich]." Grove Music Online. Accessed June 13, 2021. https://doi.org/10.1093/gmo/9781561592630.article.40060.

Hobgood, Allison. *Beholding Disability in Renaissance England*. Ann Arbor, MI: University of Michigan Press, 2021.

Holman, Peter and Paul O'Dette. "Downland, John." Grove Music Online. Accessed June 8, 2021. https://doi.org/10.1093/gmo/9781561592630.article.08103.

Howe, Blake, Stephanie Jensen-Moulton, Joseph N. Straus, Jennifer Iverson, Jessica A. Holmes, Michael B. Bakan, Andrew Dell'Antonio, and Elizabeth J. Grace. "On the Disability Aesthetics of Music." *Journal of the American Musicological Society* 69, no. 2 (2016): 525–563. https://doi-org.pallas2.tcl.sc.edu/10.1525/jams.2016.69.2.525.

Howe, Blake, Stephanie Jensen-Moulton, Neil Lerner, and Joseph Straus. *The Oxford Handbook of Music and Disability Studies*. New York: Oxford University Press, 2015.

Hunter, David. "Handel's Ill Health: Documents and Diagnoses." *Royal Musical Association Research Chronicle*, no. 41 (2008): 69–92.

Johnson, Shersten. "Notational Systems and Conceptualizing Music: A Case Study of Print and Braille Notation." *Music Theory Online* 15, no. 3–4. Accessed July 14, 2021. https://mtosmt.org/issues/mto.09.15.3/mto.09.15.3.johnson.html.

Kerman, Joseph. *Contemplating Music: Challenges to Musicology*. Cambridge, MA: Harvard University Press, 1985.

Kerman, Joseph, Alan Tyson, Scott G. Burnham, Douglas Johnson, and William Drabkin. "Beethoven, Ludwig van." Grove Music Online. Accessed July 2, 2021. https://doi.org/10.1093/gmo/9781561592630.article.40026.

Keynes, Milo. "Handel and His Illness." *The Musical Times* 123, no. 1675 (1982): 613–614.

Kleege, Georgina. "Blindness and Visual Culture: An Eyewitness Account." In *The Disability Studies Reader*, 4th edition, edited by Lennard J. Davis, 447–455. New York: Routledge, 2013.

Law, Hedy. "A Cannon-Shaped Man with an Amphibian Voice: Castrato and Disability in Eighteenth-Century France." In *The Oxford Handbook of Music and Disability Studies*, edited by Blake Howe, Stephanie Jensen-Moulton, Neil Lerner, and Joseph Straus, 329–344. New York: Oxford University Press, 2015. https://doi.org/10.1093/oxfordhb/9780199331444.013.11.

Lerner, Neil and Joseph Straus. *Sounding Off: Theorizing Disability in Music*. New York: Routledge, 2006.

Locke, Arthur Ware, and E. T. A. Hoffmann, "Beethoven's Instrumental Music: Translated from E. T. A. Hoffmann's "Kreisleriana" with an Introductory Note," *The Musical Quarterly* 3, no. 1 (1917): 123–133. http://www.jstor.org/stable/738009.

Lubet, Alex. *Music, Disability, and Society*. Philadelphia, PA: Temple University Press, 2011.

Lukin, Josh. "Disability and Blackness." In *The Disability Studies Reader*, 4th edition, edited by Lennard J. Davis, 308–315. New York: Routledge, 2013.

McClary, Susan. *Feminine Endings*. Minneapolis, MN: University of Minnesota Press, 1991.

Metzler, Irina. *A Social History of Disability in the Middle Ages: Cultural Considerations of Physical Impairment*. New York: Routledge, 2013.

Morrison, Susan Signe. *A Medieval Woman's Companion: Women's Lives in the European Middle Ages*. Havertown, PA: Oxbow Books, 2015.

Palisca, Claude V. "Baroque." Grove Music Online. Accessed June 13, 2021. https://doi.org/10.1093/gmo/9781561592630.article.02097.

———. "Zarlino, Gioseffo." Grove Music Online. Accessed June 8, 2021. https://doi.org/10.1093/gmo/9781561592630.article.30858.

Radano, Ronald and Philip Bohlman. *Music and the Racial Imagination*. Chicago, IL: The University of Chicago Press, 2000.

Ranft, Patricia. "Ruminations on Hildegard of Bingen (1098–1179) and Autism." *Journal of Medical Biography* 22, no. 2 (2014): 107–115, https://doi.org/10.1177/0967772013479283.

Rowden, Terry. *The Songs of Blind Folk: African American Musicians and the Cultures of Blindness*. Ann Arbor, MI: University of Michigan Press, 2009.

Ruud, Jay. 2014. "Scivias." In *Encyclopedia of Medieval Literature*, 2nd edition. Accessed October 25, 2021. https://login.pallas2.tcl.sc.edu/login?url=https://search.credoreference.com/content/entry/fofmedieval/scivias/0?institutionId=6481.

Sacks, Oliver. *Migraine: Revised and Expanded*. New York: Vintage Books, 1992.

Schiersari, Juliana. *The Gendering of Melancholia*. Ithaca, NY: Cornell University Press, 1992.

Schweik, Susan M., and Robert A. Wilson. "Ugly Laws." February 5, 2015 https://eugenicsarchive.ca/discover/connections/54d39e27f8a0ea47060.

Shakespeare, Tom. "The Social Model of Disability." In *The Disability Studies Reader*, 4th edition, edited by Lennard J. Davis, 214–221. New York: Routledge, 2013.

Singer, Charles. *Studies in the History and Method of Science*. Oxford: Clarendon Press, 1917.

Singer, Julie. "Playing by Ear: Compensation, Reclamation, and Prosthesis in Fourteenth-Century Song." In *Disability in the Middle Ages: Reconsiderations and Reverberations*, edited by Joshua R. Eyler, 39–52. Burlington, VT: Ashgate Publishing Company, 2010.

Snyder, Sharon L., and David T. Mitchell. *Narrative Prosthesis: Disability and Its Dependencies of Discourse*. Ann Arbor, MI: University of Michigan Press, 2000.

Solie, Ruth. *Musicology and Difference: Gender and Sexuality in Music Scholarship*. Berkeley, CA: University of California Press, 1993.

"Squarcialupi Codex." Music for the Eyes: Manuscripts from the Frank Cooper Music Facsimile Collection. University of Miami. Accessed May 25, 2020. http://scholar.library.miami.edu/facsimile/squarcialupi.html.

Straus, Joseph N. *Broken Beauty: Musical Modernism and the Representation of Disability*. New York: Oxford University Press, 2018.

———. "Disability in "Late Style" Music." The Cuny Graduate Center. Accessed November 5, 2021. https://academicworks.cuny.edu/gc_pubs/417/.

———. *Extraordinary Measures: Disability in Music*. New York: Oxford University Press, 2011.

Tarkkanen, Ahti. "Blindness of Johann Sebastian Bach." *Acta Ophthalmologica* 91 (2013): 191–192.

Tråvén, Marianne. "Voicing the Third Gender: The Castrato Voice and the Stigma of Emasculation in Eighteenth-Century Society." *Études Épistémè* 29 (2016). https://doi.org/10.4000/episteme.1220.

Turner, David M. *Disability in Eighteenth-Century England: Imagining Physical Impairment*. New York: Routledge, 2012.

Wallace, Robin. *Hearing Beethoven: A Story of Musical Loss and Discovery*. Chicago, IL: University of Chicago Press, 2018.

Walsh, Stephen. "Stravinsky, Igor (Fyodorovich)." Grove Music Online. Accessed July 14, 2021. https://doi.org/10.1093/gmo/9781561592630.article.52818.

Wheatley, Edward. *Stumbling Blocks before the Blind: Medieval Constructions of a Disability*. Ann Arbor, MI: University of Michigan Press, 2010.

4 Case Studies of Disabled Composers and Musicians in Popular Music

Disability occupies a central place within popular music discourse. As disability studies and popular music scholar George McKay argues, "There are identifiable and powerful links between popular music and the damaged, imperfect, deviant, extraordinary body or voice, which can be, and surprisingly often is, a disabled body or voice."[1] In short, disability is ubiquitous within and intrinsic to popular music genres. From the blues, jazz, and rhythm and blues (R&B) to rock 'n' roll, pop, hip hop, and country music, disabled musicians have encoded their experiences into popular music. Thus, we argue that popular music provides a kaleidoscopic view of the disabled experience broadly defined. The case studies herein reflect this breadth, covering topics of visible physical disability such as blindness, polio, amputation, and paraplegia, as well as invisible disabilities related to mental health, addiction, and substance use. Though the latter categories have historically been either medicalized as illnesses or stigmatized as moral failings,[2] scholars across disciplines are beginning to view these categories as part of the larger umbrella of disability.[3] Even outside academia, substance use and mental health are increasingly part of the discourse surrounding popular music. Thus, it is important for instructors to provide students with the tools to understand and analyze how disability shapes and is reflected in popular music genres.

In addition to examining disability as it relates to the lives and careers of popular musicians, it is also essential for students to understand the role the music industry plays in constructing and promoting performances of disability. The pages of popular music history are filled with the narratives of disabled performers, musicians who cultivate a disabled performance aesthetic, and an industry that often creates a disabling environment for its inhabitants. Interestingly, it is this very deviation from societal expectations via the overly sexualized body, the "genderly or sexually ambivalent body,"[4] the racially fetishized body, and the disabled body that, to quote rapper Sir Mix-A-Lot, has audiences "hooked" and they "can't stop starin."

DOI: 10.4324/9781003222224-5

It is perhaps unsurprising then that the performance of disability, the politics of staring,[5] and the display of the extraordinary body are all essential aspects of popular music and are integral to the ways audiences and scholars understand and consume this media.

The Blues

In many ways, the blues is the bedrock of twentieth-century American popular musical culture. The 12-bar form and repeated I-IV-V chord structure, the raw vocal and twangy guitar timbres, the emotive pitch-bending in the form of "blue notes," and the lyrical centrality of the everyday lived experiences of Black folks are not only intrinsic to the blues, but have also influenced the style and development of many popular American musical genres, from jazz and gospel to rock and roll, soul, and funk.[6] Interestingly, this genre, which has provided the foundation for so much of popular music culture in the twentieth and twenty-first centuries, is rooted in experiences of disability. According to Francis Davis, though the blues partially emerged from field hollers and work songs, "its first performers were men exempt from picking cotton by virtue of blindness or some other physical handicap."[7] Thus, from the beginning disability has been interwoven into the very fabric of the blues and that of American popular music more broadly, as has the experience and culture of African and African Americans.

As Davis points out, blindness was prevalent among early blues musicians and was essential to the blues mythology of the blind musical genius. This legacy has its origins in ancient Greece with the blind bard Homer and has been reaffirmed throughout history with musicians from Francesco Landini to Ray Charles. This trope is particularly pervasive in the blues tradition as evidenced from the popularity of "Blind Lemon Jefferson, Blind Boy Fuller, Sleepy John Estes, Willie McTell, Sonny Terry, Willie Johnson, Rev. Gary Davis, and Arthur Blake," who were all "crucial figures in establishing the blues as a distinctive and influential mode of popular music in America."[8] In fact, Terry Rowden comments on this phenomenon, stating that "from approximately 1920 to 1945, the word 'blind' functioned as a professional surname for a startling number of African American musicians."[9] For the most part, this epithet was attributed to these musicians by record companies, who conceptualized blindness as a marker of musical authenticity for blues musicians, though most of these musicians did not wish to be identified by their disability.

The number of blind Black blues musicians in the early twentieth century highlights the social and economic disparity between Black and White Americans, the former of whom were routinely denied access to reliable and affordable medical care. As a result, blindness and other health issues were widespread among poor Black (and often rural) communities.[10] In many ways, blindness, blackness, and marginalization were inextricably linked in the blues tradition: "Sightlessness thus becomes a version of blackness, a mark by which the dominant culture can categorize and exclude its disfranchised."[11] Yet, the music of Black blind blues musicians often counters these images of powerlessness by claiming musical and narrative agency.

Case Studies: Blind Lemon Jefferson, Bessie Smith, and Amy Winehouse

The life and career of Blind Lemon Jefferson (1893–1929) offers a prime example of one such counter-narrative. Jefferson was an important figure in blues and disability history for several reasons. Firstly, he is perhaps the most influential male blues musician ever to be recorded.[12] According to Rowden, Jefferson's performances ushered in a new era of blues music, effectively creating "the demand for the country blues that essentially signaled the end of the commercial dominance of the female 'classic' blues singers."[13] This can be heard most clearly in his vocal style and timbre, which simultaneously has a flexibility in the way he transitions between tessituras and a tightness in the higher registers that creates the characteristic crying sound of country blues.[14] In addition to shaping popular taste and paving the way for future country blues performers, Jefferson is even more notable for his independence. However, his level of self-sufficiency often caused people to doubt whether or not he was actually blind.[15]

Biographical evidence indicates that Jefferson was indeed born blind and likely did not have any functional vision. However, the skepticism surrounding Jefferson's status as a blind man due to his agency demonstrates the ways in which early blues audiences (and, indeed, people today) often equated blindness and disability with helplessness. It was this very perception of the disempowered blind Black musician that allowed early recording companies to take advantage of these performers both personally and financially. While such exploitation was and is still an entrenched characteristic of the music industry, Jefferson resisted this narrative by maintaining control of his personal and professional decisions.[16] Thus, in a society invested in and dependent upon the powerlessness of Black people, Jefferson acted as a foil to ableist perceptions of blindness and bigoted views of Black men by musically voicing the independence and agency of blind blues musicians.

Though male blind blues singers have become a trope of the genre, blind female blues singers are rarely discussed in blues scholarship. In fact, few blind women had careers as blues performers. This was due in large part to the perception of blind women as vulnerable to abuse and thus they were often discouraged from pursuing work opportunities in the public sphere.

There are exceptions to this, with the Memphis street singer, Blind Mamie Forehand, as the most notable. However, that she often performed alongside her husband, A.C. Forehand, reinforces the notion that blind women are somehow more vulnerable than other populations and in need of special protection.[17] This double standard in popular music persists today and is an important topic of discussion for students to consider.

Despite the relative absence of famous blind female musicians, there are certainly other instances of female performers with disabilities in this genre. This is especially evident when considering the prevalence of substance use and addiction within the blues tradition (and popular music more broadly). Perhaps one of the most legendary blues figures to experience addiction was **Bessie Smith (1894–1937)**. Smith is a crucial figure in the history of blues whose career offers a window into the social, cultural, and racial landscape of the early twentieth century in the United States. Smith was born in Chattanooga, Tennessee, and began performing on East Ninth Street, the city's African American center for entertainment and commerce.[18] In 1912, she transitioned from an amateur street performer to a professional singer on a vaudeville circuit, notably singing in the same show as Gertrude "Ma" Rainey.[19] For the next few years, Smith continued performing in minstrel shows and cabarets before rocketing to stardom with her 1923 recording of *Downhearted Blues*.

Smith's slow, broad phrasing, wide range, and fine intonation coupled with her raw vocal timbre established her as the premiere jazz-blues singer of the 1920s and earned her the epithet, the "Empress of Blues."[20] During this time she made over 200 recordings and was the highest paid Black performing artist in the United States. Yet, this success was tempered with Smith's struggle with alcoholism and separation from her husband in 1929.[21] By the beginning of the 1930s, Smith's career rapidly declined due to a shifting preference for jazz among audiences. This change in public taste coincided with an increasing severity of her addiction, which began to affect her consistency and reliability as a performer and led to intermittent periods of financial hardship.[22]

Many of Smith's songs explore the role of alcohol in her life and the lives of Black women, as heard in her hits "Gimme a Pigfoot and a Bottle of Beer," "Me and My Gin," and "Gin House Blues." The latter weaves together a narrative of a woman who goes to the gin house following a long day of work, seeking an escape from an unhappy relationship and hoping to drown her sorrows in gin and the company of a stranger. Here Smith provides her audience with insight into the life of a working-class African American woman who attempts to mitigate daily oppression and mistreatment through substance use. This song highlights the struggles Smith faced as an African American bisexual woman with a disability. Yet, even as she sings these plaintive verses, her tone and the lyrics themselves are full of agency: "I'll make one trip there to seek and ease my mind / And if I do, I'm gonna make it / My last time." As with many of her songs, "Gin House Blues," presents an unapologetic picture of Smith's life as a blues woman attempting to navigate her complex identities that intersect at the crossroads of race, sexuality, gender, and disability.

Smith's legacy has lived on through the voices of both Black and white female singers who she inspired such as Billie Holiday, Janis Joplin, and Laura Nyro.[23] Perhaps one of the most compelling examples of Smith's influence can be heard in the vocal stylings of British singer **Amy Winehouse (1983–2011)**.[24] In many ways, Winehouse's vocal style defies and transgresses genre boundaries. As stated by critic Sasha Frere-Jones, Winehouse has elements "of the girl groups of the sixties, the jazz singers of the forties, and a variety of rhythms from the seventies and the nineties."[25] However, it is important to unpack this mélange of musical influences, particularly given Winehouse's identity as a white woman engaging in "a kind of sonic blue(s)face performance."[26] Her pastiche of R&B, soul, jazz, blues, and hip hop mixed with her own idiosyncratic vocal timbre and slurred dialect firmly place Winehouse in a long line of white and Black female singers engaged in the "performative tactics of musical minstrelsy."[27] This is perhaps most evident in Winehouse's Grammy-award winning album, *Back to Black* (2008), which features witty and cutting lyrics backed by the retro-soul Brooklyn-based band, Dap-Kings.

Yet, the title of the album refers less to Winehouse's engagement with the "culture of aural racial mimicry"[28] than it does to Winehouse's struggles with addiction. Though separated by over five decades, the lives of Smith and Winehouse have striking parallels, not only in their vocal styles, but in their identities as female singers whose disability relative to addiction shaped their careers. Throughout her life, Winehouse experienced mental health issues ranging from depression to eating disorders and openly admitted to using alcohol and drugs as coping mechanisms: "The more insecure I feel, the more I drink."[29] Just as many people pointed to Smith's alcoholism as a major factor in the decline of her career, so too have critics alike patently declared that Winehouse was killed by her addictions. However, to dismiss Winehouse as yet another member of the 27 Club would be reductive.[30]

In order to fully understand Winehouse's musical identity as it relates to her impairment, we must take an intersectional approach. However, in addition to gender and race, we must also examine the role of the entertainment industry as a disabling culture that promotes pressures and temptations for economic profit. As McKay points out, "Pop stardom is an illness that can seriously, even fatally, threaten health and undermine ability; to do well in this career is frequently to be or to get a bit or a lot fucked up."³¹ In this way, success in the popular music industry is predicated on a performance of disability. This aligns closely with the trope of pop music as a realm governed by "sex, drugs, and rock and roll." It is no wonder then that Smith sang about "Me and My Gin," nor that her twenty-first-century heir-apparent, Amy Winehouse, won praise for her song "Rehab," in which she refuses treatment for both her addiction and her interrelated depression. "Rehab" not only reveals the prevalence of the medical model within the music industry, in which rehab is the norm, but also the ways in which the *need* for rehab is expected. Rather than sensationalizing musical drug culture, this allows students and instructors to examine how Winehouse's disability and the pressures of the performing industry are co-constructed and represented in her music. The lives and careers of Smith and Winehouse offer us important opportunities to reflect on our role as cultural consumers in either contributing to or speaking out against exploitative environments in which disability is simultaneously rewarded and punished.

Additional Reading/Listening for Students

Lower, Jonathan. "Teaching Disability into History: History, Disability Studies and Blues Music." *Teaching United States History*. Accessed July 21, 2021. http://www.teachingushistory.co/2019/09/teaching-disability-into-history-history-disability-studies-and-blues-music.html.

Thompkins, Gwen. "Forebears: Bessie Smith, The Empress Of The Blues." *NPR*, January 5, 2018, https://www.npr.org/2018/01/05/575422226/forebears-bessie-smith-the-empress-of-the-blues.

Jazz

Much like the blues, jazz is a genre that has provided a foundation for the development of popular music in the twentieth century. This is evident through both its reputation as a "quintessential American art form,"³² as well as its ubiquity in the global soundscape.³³ However, at its inception, jazz was marginalized as a form of sonic pathology, rather than viewed as a budding music genre. As musicologist Laurie Stras points out, "In the 1920s and 1930s, jazz was indeed 'disabled' music', considered by many to be aesthetically and functionally impaired to the point that it not only served no purpose, but also was an active agent of medical and social disorder."³⁴

It was not just the subject matter of jazz, which often focused on romantic relationships and sex, but also the musical structure, featuring melodies rife with syncopation, that caused a primarily white audience base and music industry to view jazz as non-normative and therefore disabled. This notion of disability as a form of deviation was promoted through the medical model of disability, which dominated discourse on disability during the first half of the twentieth century. The medical model not only viewed impairment as a problem in need of remediation but contextualized disability as a form of loss. This narrative gained considerable traction as acquired disability, through industrial accidents, survival of disease, and trauma as a result of World War I, became nearly ubiquitous.[35] Seen through this lens, jazz was not only a disabled form of music, but represented a departure from "good," "whole," and "normative" musical genres of the time.

It is no coincidence that this so-called "disabled" music was pioneered by African American musicians, who were routinely "Othered" by white audiences. This marginalization of African Americans took place both through political segregation policies, such as the Jim Crow Laws, as well as through the appropriation and misrepresentation of African American musical culture in stereotypical performances of Blackface minstrelsy.[36] The pattern of demeaning and then co-opting African American musical forms was repeated with jazz, as can be seen from the initial dismissal of the genre in the 1920s and then its rise in popularity among white audiences in the 1930s and 1940s. In addition to the mutually reinforcing ableist and racist rhetoric that shaped this genre, jazz also has a very literal connection to disability. Much like the blues, many famous jazz performers are also disabled. Though addiction and substance use are certainly a shared characteristic between these two genres, this section will focus on performers with physical disabilities. While the interconnectivity of race and disability to the history and construction of jazz can be challenging to unpack with students, the following case studies provide accessible examples of how disabled jazz musicians have either served to reinforce or challenge tropes of disability and race within jazz music.

Case Studies: Connie Boswell, Art Tatum, and Django Reinhardt

One early performer who helped popularize jazz among white audiences was **Connie Boswell (1907–1976)**, a wheelchair user who became permanently disabled as a result of polio. She began her career as part of a trio in the 1920s, performing alongside her sisters Martha and Vet. The Boswell Sisters hailed from New Orleans, Louisiana, where they grew up listening to blues music. These sounds shaped their own vocal stylings, which showcased their naturally lower tessituras and southern diction and featured heavily syncopated rhythms and scat singing.[37] Though the Boswell Sisters were white, these musical characteristics combined with their dark hair and eyes led radio audiences to frequently question their racial identity. In this way, their vocal style crossed racial boundaries. Yet, given their upbringing in New Orleans and their carefully cultivated self-image as "southern belles," their sound marked a departure from the minstrel-inflected performances that attempted to co-opt and ridicule African American culture.[38] At a time when jazz was perceived as a "disabled" and non-normative musical form by mainstream audiences, the Boswell Sisters succeeded in creating "commercially viable" arrangements, effectively "destigmatising the music and opening its appreciation to the wider American public."[39]

The trio disbanded in 1936 due to Martha and Vet's desire to begin families. Connie, who was also recently married, used this opportunity to launch her solo career. Connie Boswell quickly became one of the most influential singers of her generation. Her vocal style, marked by "loose, drawling diction; a more speechlike, naturally emotive delivery; and a lower, mellower tone and tessitura" helped shape the sound of jazz and influenced singers such as Bing Crosby and Ella Fitzgerald.[40] During her career, Boswell worked in all performing mediums, including radio, television, and film. In these more visual forms of media, Boswell always performed in a seated position, perhaps to downplay the visibility of her disability. However, the fact that she was a wheelchair user was widely known yet did not seem to negatively impact her career. Musicologist Laurie Stras argues that the longevity of Boswell's career and mainstream audiences' repeated exposure to Boswell and jazz across media helped to mitigate her "Otherness" as a disabled, southern, and jazz performer. In this way, Boswell's multidecade success in the recording and television industries offers insight into the role of repetition in minimizing difference. Moreover, it underscores the importance of increasing representation of disability in order to combat the stigmatization of marginalized populations. Despite the importance of her contributions to the popular music industry, in many ways Boswell represents the "exception to the rule" in that she was the "only visibly disabled 'A-list' female popular entertainer for most of the twentieth century."[41] This fact highlights the exclusive nature of the popular music industry that persists to the present day.

Boswell was not the only disabled jazz performer to be viewed through the lens of exceptionalism. In fact, this narrative is often applied to blind jazz musicians. While blindness was fairly ubiquitous among blues musicians, far fewer jazz performers were blind. This was due to a combination of greater access to medical care among African Americans in the 1920s and 1930s as well as the fact that the urban environments in which jazz was cultivated were far more challenging for blind musicians to negotiate.[42] The declining incidence of blindness combined with the increasing number of career opportunities for blind folks caused people to conceptualize blind jazz performers as "exceptions."[43] Two major stereotypes have been used to explain the success of blind performers in both the blues and jazz and to characterize them as "geniuses": (1) the "super crip," "someone who overcomes their disability in ways that are often seen by the public as inspiring";[44] (2) "the superstition of sensory compensation," the belief that the loss of one sense leads to the improvement of another.[45]

The trope of the blind jazz genius has been applied to several artists throughout history, such as Ray Charles and Rasaan Roland Kirk, but is perhaps most evident when examining the life and career of **Arthur (Art) Tatum (1909–1956)**. Tatum was born blind in one eye with partial sight in the other, making him legally blind. As a teenager he studied piano at the Toledo School of Music and learned songs through a mixture of music notation via Braille music and aural methods, such as listening to the radio, piano rolls, and other musicians.[46] Yet, unlike many musicians before him whose musical reputation was closely tied to the novelty of their blindness, Tatum cultivated a reputation as a virtuoso.[47] To this day, Tatum's technical abilities remain the stuff of legend. According to Howlett and Robinson, this was due not only to his physical dexterity, but also to his improvisatory style and "seemingly unlimited capacity to expand and enrich a melody and a profound and continually evolving grasp of substitute harmonies."[48]

His 600 recordings made over the course of his career document his highly ornamental and innovative style. Interestingly, he rarely composed his own music, preferring instead to perform jazz and blues standards. This focus on standard repertoire was disparaged by some critics who argued that Tatum's characteristic style had become predictable and demonstrated a lack of growth.[49] Perhaps a more productive way to understand Tatum's style is not through an absence of dynamism, but a presence of isolation. Though he could often "pass" as sighted, his blindness did present challenges to living an "independent" life in a society than increasingly privileged individualism as a social and creative ideal. Furthermore, one could argue that the superiority of Tatum's playing relative to contemporary and future pianists served as another source of isolation. Though he inspired future generations, such as Bud Powell, Lennie Tristano, and Herbie Hancock who attempted to learn Tatum performances by rote, few had the skill to replicate his virtuosic technique.[50] Tatum is indisputably a formative figure within jazz, and yet, his identity as a blind musical genius seems to create a narrative that runs parallel to rather than being integrated within jazz history. It is both his blindness and his unmatched virtuosity that have simultaneously caused jazz musicians to idealize and dismiss Tatum, serving as a reminder that a pedestal is its own kind of margin.

Frequently cited as the "Father of Gypsy Jazz," **Jean "Django" Reinhardt (1910–1953)** was born into a family of traveling Manouche Gypsy entertainers.[51] He lived the archetypical Bohemian existence that included traveling throughout Europe, learning to play the guitar, violin, and banjo, and eventually performing alongside caravan parties. He was only 12 years old when he began performing in small ensembles playing the banjo-guitar in French cafes. In 1928, Reinhardt was involved in a caravan fire that significantly damaged his left hand, particularly his pinky and ring finger, and left leg. His surgeon wanted to amputate his leg in order to avoid gangrene, but Reinhardt refused and opted for a long and arduous rehabilitation instead. During this time, he relearned to play the guitar without full use of his pinky and ring finger, though there has been much debate about whether he had any function in these digits. Some scholars claim that his fingers were mangled and/or disfigured, rendering them useless in his guitar playing. Others claim he had some limited function of those fingers. This continued debate among music historians brings to bear the very mystique of his musical legacy: was Reinhardt's musicality a direct result of his impairment and need to adapt his playing technique, or was it due to his raw talent and Roma influence?[52] So much of Reinhardt's legacy is heavily entrenched in the overcoming narrative. One way to aid students in challenging the trope of "overcoming" disability is to examine Reinhardt's Roma identity. This provides students with a unique opportunity to explore the intersections of the overcoming narrative, the misguided equation of impairment and brilliance, and the musical culture of the historically oppressed Roma people through the life and music of Django Reinhardt.

As suggested above, there are other notable aspects of Reinhardt's identity that are critical to contextualizing his place in the annals of music history. Reinhardt lived in Europe during World War II and the Holocaust, where the Roma were persecuted by Hitler and the Nazis alongside Jewish people, Communists, Catholics, disabled people, and queer men. Furthermore, he continued to perform in Nazi-occupied Paris despite Hitler's declaration that jazz music was deemed "degenerate" due to its association with Black and Jewish people. Even with the formal banning of jazz by Hitler and Joseph Goebbels, Minister of Public Enlightenment and Propaganda, jazz was immensely popular, even among Nazi officers.[53] This meant that Reinhardt and other artists continued to perform while under the constant threat of danger. The intersection of Reinhardt's identities of Roma, jazz musician, and disabled person highlights the multidimensionality that both enriches and complicates this musical narrative as presented to students of today. Thus, rather than attempting to simplify and reduce Reinhardt's legacy to questions of functionality brought on by his impairment, it is incumbent upon us as pedagogues to view his music within the interconnected web of disability, ethnicity, and class to counteract narratives of overcoming and "Othering."

Additional Reading/Listening for Students

"Art Tatum - Yesterdays 1954." *YouTube* 2, no. 17 (October 12, 2012). https://www.youtube.com/watch?v=q0QD558TWSQ.

Burnett, John. "Art Tatum: A Talent Never to Be Duplicated." *NPR*, November 5, 2006, https://www.npr.org/templates/story/story.php?storyId=6434701.

"Connee Boswell, Lee Phillip—1963 TV Interview, Polio." *YouTube Video* 14, no. 14. (December 26, 2015). https://www.youtube.com/watch?v=z0Rk_ugoi58.

"Django Reinhardt-Minor Swing-HD*1080p." *YouTube* 3, no. 16 (March 28, 2013). https://www.youtube.com/watch?v=gcE1avXFJb4.

Dregni, Michael. *Django: The Life and Music of a Gypsy Legend.* New York: Oxford University Press, 2006.

Rhythm and Blues, Rock and Roll, and Pop Music

Though rhythm and blues, rock and roll, and pop music all are distinct genres within the umbrella of vernacular music, there are many points of intersection relative to expectations of performativity, cultivation of image, musical characteristics, and the pervasiveness of disability. Thus, this subsection combines discussions of these three genres and explores a variety of disabled identities that spans the gamut from physical disabilities, such as paraplegia and blindness, to "invisible" mental health concerns, including bipolar disorder and substance use. It is important to note that while this section offers five case studies of well-known disabled musicians, there are and have been countless others within the popular music industry.[54]

As the name would suggest, rhythm and blues (R&B) is an outgrowth of the blues genre inflected by big band jazz aesthetics and gospel music. These styles, which were championed by African American artists in the first half of the twentieth century, coalesced to create a new genre that changed the sound of popular music. In fact, the sound of "saxophones, pounding pianos, and red-hot electric guitars" and a Gospel style of singing that characterizes R&B heavily influenced "the foundations of rock-and-roll music played by Chuck Berry, Elvis Presley, and Little Richard in the mid-1950s."[55] The connection between R&B and rock and roll is not only evident in these musical characteristics, but also in the crossover success of some of its most famous artists, such as Ray Charles and Teddy Pendergrass.

Case Studies: Ray Charles, Teddy Pendergrass, Britney Spears, and Lady Gaga

Born Ray Charles Robinson, the tale of **Ray Charles (1930–2004)**, the Genius of Soul, is a convoluted fusion of blindness, blackness, substance abuse, and musical brilliance shrouded in tropes of blind mysticism, the rhetoric of genius,[56] and the overcoming narrative. Charles indirectly credits his perspective on blindness to the fact that he had seven years of sight to carry with him. Though Charles was often honest about his experience of blindness when asked, he seemed to purposely leave it out of his narrative whenever possible. Terry Rowden discusses Charles' reference to his own blindness as a kind of "rejection of identification," a term coined by blind activists. For Charles this manifested through a focus on his musical career, rather than using his position to advocate for the blind community. Indeed, the most obvious marker of his blindness was his iconic sunglasses, which only contributed to his mystique as a blind and Black musician and in many ways served to make him more attractive and glamorous.

Charles effortlessly blended musical genres such as soul, rock 'n' roll, jazz, gospel, blues, and country and western. His tenure with Atlantic Records actualized new and exciting music that challenged racial codes and traditional musical genres. With hit songs like "Hallelujah, I Love Her So," "I Got a Woman," "Hit the Road Jack," and "What'd I Say," it is easy to see why Charles is so frequently cited as the "Genius of Soul." Although he typically rejected the title, this rhetoric of genius is a significant part of his legacy. Interestingly though, Charles' genre bending was not always interpreted as artistic genius. To some music critics, this trademark came off as inauthentic or even sacrilegious to the Gospel music he often emulated. This deviation from sacred Gospel music led to musicologists typically placing him outside of the Black musical mainstream.[57] However, his blackness, blindness, musical imitation skills, and handsomeness positioned him as one of the few Black or blind performers to have regular access to TV audiences where he "was faced with the challenge of providing an unthreatening image of both blackness and blindness for audiences who were generally uncomfortable with the former and increasingly unfamiliar with the latter."[58]

Though Charles began using heroin at the age of 18, his arrest in 1965 for possession of heroin and marijuana ended up serving as a crossroads for him. To avoid jail time, he agreed to go to rehab and by 1966 he was ready to restart his musical career. In his autobiography, *Brother Ray*, he speaks candidly about his experience of addiction. Substance abuse is often associated with the blues and the artists who helped define the genre.[59] While Charles was transparent about his long usage of heroin, he worked to prevent it from dominating his narrative and legacy.[60]

Much like Charles, **Teddy Pendergrass (1950–2010)** grew up in the musical environment of the church and later joined the Philadelphia Boys Choir and All City School Choir during grade school and junior high.[61] At age 19, he joined a singing group called the Blue Notes, which later created the hit songs "If You Don't Know Me By Now," "The Love I Lost," and "Wake Up Everybody."[62] In 1975, Pendergrass launched his solo career and two years later his first album went platinum. Pendergrass established himself as one of the premiere soul singers of the decade and gained widespread popularity, particularly among female audiences. His performance of "black masculine heterosexuality" was communicated through his "characteristically deep voice" and "a repertoire of late-night seductive and romantic soul music."[63] This performance of Black masculinity elevated him to the status of a sex symbol among his fans, which was reinforced through his women-only concerts. However, this identity was challenged after he sustained a spinal cord injury from a car accident in 1982 and subsequently became paraplegic.[64] Pendergrass describes that he was initially "devastated" by the accident,[65] particularly after a newspaper article remarked that Pendergrass' career was over because "If he sang from a wheelchair, it wouldn't be the same."[66]

Despite this experience of public rejection, Pendergrass returned to the stage in 1985 at the Live Aid concert in Philadelphia singing "Reach Out and Touch (Somebody's Hand)." Though the concert was a great success, Pendergrass subsequently stopped performing for a time due to medical complications and drug and alcohol use. He chronicles his journey in the autobiography *Truly Blessed* (1998), in which he explores his challenges and triumphs through his transformation from an able-bodied soul-singing sex symbol to a paraplegic musician, author, and disability advocate. It is notable that though his disability changed his life considerably, Pendergrass still continued to perform sexual love songs, offering a counter-narrative to the myth that people with disabilities are not sexual beings. In so doing, Pendergrass demonstrated that people with physical disabilities are and can be "the object of romantic, erotic interest."[67] Though Pendergrass largely succeeded in shaping the narrative of his disability, many artists with impairments are further marginalized by a disabling entertainment industry and stigmatizing public. This is especially evident in the genre of pop music, where consumers play a significant role in either reinforcing or rejecting ableist expectations for artists. Two important examples of this can be seen through the lives and careers of Britney Spears and Lady Gaga.

From Mouseketeer in 1993 to America's "Princess of Pop" by 1998, **Britney Spears (1981–)** has monopolized the popular music/cultural landscape since her breakout hit of "...Baby one more time" in 1998. Her rise to fame, fall from the top, and multiple comebacks have kept her as one of the media's favorite storylines.[68] Spears' career trajectory has been complicated by her mental health diagnoses of bipolar disorder and anxiety and depression, and the media's damaging quest to first expose it and then project it. Musically speaking, Spears hit her stride with the demand for bubblegum pop music in the late 1990s and early 2000s. Due to her immense album successes, she has been ranked as the best-selling female artist in the United States by the Recording Industry Association of America.

As with any popular star of this stature, Spears' personal life was played out for the public to dissect, theorize, and pathologize.[69] The mid to late 2000s proved to be an emotionally exhausting time period in Spears' life: she entered into two unsuccessful marriages, had two children, went to rehab, was involuntarily hospitalized, and lost full custody of her children. While the world watched her publicly unravel, her parents, Jamie and Lynne, pushed for the conservatorship that controlled Spears' life until 2021. The conservatorship was divided into two parts: (1) her estate, which included her income and all financial decisions, and (2) her person, which related to her well-being and health.[70] She shared that regardless of her mental health she was forced to perform, use birth control, and take medication against her will. This plays into the long history of disabled people being controlled by so-called "keepers" who restricted their agency and reproductive rights.[71]

Born out of disgust over Spears' lack of autonomy, avid fans took to social media creating the #Free-Britney movement to raise awareness of the conservatorship that began in 2019. The outrage over the strict terms of her conservatorship was both necessary and warranted, and it represents a drastic shift in popular opinion about Spears and her public battle with mental health. Spears' embrace of being bipolar along with advocating for personal and financial freedom align with the tenets of the Mad Pride Movement. Mad Pride activists "believe mainstream psychiatry over exaggerates psychic pathology and over enforces psychic conformity in the guise of diagnostic labeling and treatment which all too often comes in the form of forced manipulated hospitalizations, restraints, seclusions, and medication."[72] In addition to advocating for the agency of individuals with mental health issues, Mad Pride seeks to overturn negative stigma about mental health. As stated by disability studies scholar Bradley Lewis

> Like the celebratory and reappropriative uses of the terms 'Crip,' 'Queer,' and 'Black Pride,' the term 'Mad Pride' overturns traditional distinctions and hierarchies. It signifies a reversal of standard pathological connotations of 'madness.' Rather than pathologizing mental difference, Mad Pride signifies a stance of respect, appreciation, and affirmation.[73]

Her forced comeback in late 2007 was laced with dangerous constructs of disability that ultimately reaffirm the overcoming narrative via the body. As Christopher R. Smit suggests: "This is the mental illness of celebrity. The context creates the pressure, the pressure creates the symptom, the symptom must be hidden from the context for it to continue. Fame demands the cloak of health."[74] Thus, the reading of disability in the work and life of Spears is not so much about her actual music but the way her impairment has been represented by the media. This provides an excellent opportunity for students to consider the pressures exerted by an ableist industry on artists to conform to normative standards of the bodymind.

On March 28, 1986, a star was born. Steffani Germanotta, publicly known as **Lady Gaga**, first began including overt representations of disability and bodily deviance into her performances with her 2008 single "Paparazzi." If ever there was a moment in popular culture that glamorized assistive technology or mobility aids, it was Gaga's use of the bedazzled wheelchair that made its initial debut in the song's accompanying music video. After "Paparazzi" came her embodiment of monstrosity in both her music and performances, the Lady Gaga Disability Project,[75] "Born this Way" (emerging as the anthem for the "Other"), and her alter ego Yüyi, a wheelchair-using mermaid she debuted in 2011.

Gaga's appropriation and performance of themes related to deviance, disability, gender, and sexuality serve as the crux of scholarly bewilderment. There are four separate frameworks from which to view Gaga's performative identities: (1) disability chic, "a process of using the different and disabled body as an element of style and message";[76] (2) Gaga Feminism, an insincere performance of femininity that critiques gender binaries;[77] (3) "empowered deviance" in which Gaga provides non-normative representations of bodily difference;[78] and (4) enfreakment, the performance of a freak aesthetic in order to promote bodily difference and disability.[79] Each of these frameworks offer different approaches for situating Gaga's performative identities. A point of contention among scholars is that Gaga often portrays disability as a prop that is both ornamental and temporary. This is problematic as it belittles the reality of disability for those permanently impaired. It also reinforces the medical model of disability by suggesting that with time and medical intervention one can shed their disability and once again occupy the space of a normative body.[80]

It is important to note that Lady Gaga publicly revealed in 2017 via Twitter that she has fibromyalgia. The tweet reads: "In our documentary the #chronicillness #chronicpain I deal w/ is #Fibromyalgia I wish to help raise awareness & connect people who have it."[81] Gaga attributed her development of fibromyalgia after a significant hip injury while performing for her *Born This Way Ball* world tour. Although Gaga had previously shared her struggles with depression and anxiety, this too became more prominent once she shared her fibromyalgia diagnosis. This revelation may shed new light on her past tokenization and glamorization of disability. However, since her transition to jazz crooner and silver screen star, previously dominant themes of disability seem to have all but vanished from her stage performances.

Case Studies in Popular Music 101

This leaves scholars and fans wondering how to reconcile with her past problematic representations of disability. In the classroom, her sensational performances that often glamorize disability and conflate gender and normativity can be used as possible topics for discussions. The following list of frameworks and specific displays of performative identities can be used when incorporating Lady Gaga into your class: (1) Her embodiment of disability chic in "Paparazzi" and the Lady Gaga Disability Project, (2) Gaga feminism as it applies to her alter ego Jo Calderone and other gender-bending acts, (3) her enfreakment of popular music through her thematic adoption of the monster, freak, and "Other," and (4) her "empowered deviance" as seen in her many non-normative performance identities.

Additional Reading/Listening for Students

Ashford &Simpson / Teddy Pendergrass. "Reach Out and Touch (Live Aid 1985)." *YouTube Video* 6, no. 11 (October 11, 2018). https://www.youtube.com/watch?v=A1QnhENzXDk.

Davisson, Amber. *Lady Gaga and the Remaking of Celebrity Culture*. Jefferson, North Carolina and London: McFarland & Company, Inc., Publishers, 2013.

Lydon, Michael. *Ray Charles: Man and Music*. New York: Riverhead Books, 1995.

Smit, Christopher R. *The Exile of Britney Spears: A Tale of 21st Century Consumption*. Bristol, UK and Chicago: Intellect, 2011.

Country

From its beginnings in the 1920s, "country" music has been a complex, multifaceted, and constantly shifting tradition. This is evident from merely examining the shifting terminology used to describe this genre, which was originally known as folk or old-time music and later became commercially marketed as "hillbilly" music before finally earning the title of "country." Yet even today country music is made up of a variety of subgenres. These are at times divided by regional identity in the examples of Texas versus Nashville sound and in other cases are demarcated by stylistic nomenclature, such as honky-tonk, alt-country, country western, and Americana. Nadine Hubb comments on this diversity in her book *Rednecks, Queers, and Country Music* stating, "the music is and always has been a hybridized, commercial cultural and media form."[82] This means that definitions of what constitutes "real" country music are highly contested and vary depending upon one's background and opinion.

One pervasive myth that dominates discourse about this genre is that country is the music of whiteness and heterosexuality; however, this is not necessarily the case (though there are large swaths of country music that speak specifically to the white, straight, blue-collar experience). In fact, narratives of country music as the sole purview of white singers and audience members are not a result of a lack of Black, Indigenous, or Latinx country artists, but are rather due to the erasure of non-white performers by the music industry both historically and today. When country music was in its nascent stages, recording labels following in the steps of the Jim Crow Laws sought to market the music of white and Black musicians separately: "During this period white southerners were labeled 'hillbilly' or 'old-time' regardless of their musical influences, while Black southerners of all stylistic stripes got clumped together under the category of 'race music.'"[83] Despite the resulting mythology of whiteness that surrounds the genre, much of country music is championed by Latinx, Black, Indigenous, and queer artists. According to Hubbs, depictions of country as the music of white, heterosexual men is "at odds with (among other things) the long presence in country music of African Americans in the South and Mexican Americans in the Southwest and the diaspora ... and the music's pivotal role in lesbian and gay two-step bars and international Gay Rodeo Association (IGRA) events."[84]

Though country music is enjoyed by members of all socioeconomic classes, historically the genre has been closely tied to working-class identity. According to Aaron Fox, "Country music is an authentic working-class art of enormous value to its blue-collar constituency."[85] This is because "country" not only serves to describe a musical genre, but is also used as a cultural and political marker of identity for "underpaid manual laborers" who represent "prototypical independent and free Americans" and "members of a functional local community."[86] Thus, country music reflects a working-class identity by embodying the working-class values of hard work, locality, and authenticity. Yet, while the labor associated with working-class life privileges images of the able-bodied, red-blooded American, the realities of working-class life are often quite disabling, as seen through the impairments acquired through hard manual labor, the lack of resources to medical care and education, and the pervasiveness of substance use and addiction to cope with physical and mental disabilities, all of which are connected to lower-levels of socioeconomic status.[87] Interestingly, though country music often speaks to these conditions, such experiences are not always perceived through the intersecting lens of disability. The following case studies offer an opportunity to explore the intersections of disability, race, class, and sexuality by comparing and contrasting the lives and careers of Hank Williams and Lil Nas X. Though these artists are separated by almost 50 years and represent dramatically different identities and styles, they both demonstrate the importance of country music in representing disabled experiences.

Case Studies: Hiram "Hank" Williams and Lil Nas X

Hiram "Hank" Williams (1923–1953), referred to as the "Hillbilly Shakespeare,"[88] was born into a poor working-class family in Mount Olive, Alabama. His father, Elonzo ("Lon"), frequently bounced from job to job working as a manual laborer and turning to alcohol to help him cope with the hardships of working-class life and the injuries he sustained from serving in World War I. His mother, Lillie, took on much of the responsibility for Williams' upbringing, particularly after forcing her husband to enter a Veterans Administration hospital in Florida as his impairment[89] grew more severe.[90] Both his father's habit of self-medicating through alcohol and his subsequent absence during Williams' formative years deeply impacted the soon-to-be "Hillbilly King." He began writing songs at age five and later explored the loneliness he felt due to his father's absence. It was this skill for showcasing emotional vulnerability that later led Williams to write such songs as "I'm So Lonesome I Could Cry," "Cold Cold Heart," and "Your Cheatin' Heart," and subsequently solidify himself as a country legend.

In addition to the emotional impact of being without his father, Williams' early life was also greatly affected by a mysterious back pain. Though Williams was taken to a medical professional, the doctor was unable to identify the impairment, assuring Williams that the pain would ebb as he grew older. It was not until years later that Williams learned he had spina bifida occulta, "a malformation of one or more of the vertebrae."[91] Today, this condition is often treated in prenatal development through supplements of folic acid. However, Williams' mother did not have the benefit of such healthcare nor was the condition widely diagnosed and treated at the time. Though spina bifida occulta is the least severe form of spina bifida, in rare cases such as Williams experienced, it can cause debilitating pain and neurological issues when the spinal cord becomes tethered. Unfortunately, Williams' pain only increased as he grew older, leading him to follow in his father's footsteps and self-medicate through both alcohol and prescription drugs.

Though he maintained a successful recording career throughout his life, Williams' alcoholism eventually affected his ability to perform live. In 1951, he underwent a spinal fusion operation that proved unsuccessful in mitigating his chronic pain. Following the surgery, he routinely took high doses of prescription drugs, such as Demerol and chloral hydrate. In 1952, he was fired from the Grand Ole Opry's radio show for his abuse of prescription drugs and alcohol; following this incident he struggled to gain bookings at larger venues and had intermittent stays in hospitals and sanatoriums.[92] While his music topped the country charts, Williams' health continued to decline and he died of an overdose of alcohol and narcotics on January 1, 1953.

Williams was 29 years old when he died, yet his short career left a lasting impact on the country music genre. In fact, Williams gained even more popularity in death than he experienced while alive, as evidenced by the 20,000 people who attended his funeral.[93] While many scholars have argued that a good deal of Williams' fame can be attributed to his short and turbulent life, he is perhaps best remembered for his vocal yodeling, falsetto style, and his gift for capturing the pain of the human experience through vulnerable songwriting. Williams has inspired subsequent generations of musicians across genres. Outside of the country genre, artists such as Dean Martin, James Brown, Louis Armstrong, Bob Dylan, Elvis Presley, and the Red Hot Chili Peppers have covered his songs while Williams remains a songwriting legend within the country world, praised for his ability to express complex emotions associated with the working-class experience in accessible language.

Williams certainly identified as belonging to the working class and incorporated this identity in his music: "Hiram Williams, like his old man, was brought up believing he was white trash–and this sensibility was his means of finding success, not by pushing it away but by turning it into engaging commercial appeal."[94] Interestingly, Williams not only encoded working-class values into his songwriting through his lyrics, which were perceived as both accessible and authentic, but also sonically communicated his experience of disability through his vocal timbre and yodeling. According to George McKay

> the falsetto is a vocal device that is notably employed by some male disabled singers, and which is understood as a sonic signification of sincerity and emotion (falsetto as truth); the expression of suffering, pain, and sensitivity (including the *falsetto*); the voicing of vulnerability (the physical effort to make and hold the note)."[95]

Here it is important to note that the aesthetics of disability and the working class are closely connected – in fact, the conditions of working-class life are often disabling, as lower socioeconomic status is tied to limited access to education, healthcare, and resource distribution. These realities of working-class life are frequently articulated through country music, which "describe(s) life as it is, not as one might wish it to be."[96] Such narratives showcase the centrality of hard work and manual labor, the importance of family as a support system (or the lack thereof), the place of emotional and physical pain, and the role of substances (alcohol specifically) in serving as a coping mechanism for dealing with the hardships of life.

In this way, themes of disability are ubiquitous within country music. A prime example can be seen in the song "Family Tradition," by Hank

Williams Jr., which emphasizes the generational history of substance use within the Williams family:

> They get on me and want to know
> Hank, why do you drink?
> Hank, why do you roll smoke?
> Why must you live out the songs that you wrote?
> Over and over
> Everybody makes my prediction
> So if I get stoned, I'm just carrying on
> An old family tradition

This brief chorus features straightforward language, yet highlights several important "truths" about disability, the working class, and country music. Firstly, country music is often encoded with experiences of disability as Williams Jr. is not only "living out the songs that [he] wrote," but sounding out the life that he lives. Secondly, he "inherited" this family tradition of substance use from his father, who used drugs and alcohol to mitigate the pain from his spina bifida, just as his father utilized alcohol to cope with chronic pain from his acquired disabilities. Thus, while substance use and addiction are disabling in and of themselves and feature prominently in country music, they often develop in response to other impairments brought on by the hardships of working-class life. In this way, the music of Hank Williams, Hank Williams Jr., and many other country artists provide important opportunities for understanding how this music highlights the intersections between disability and socioeconomic status.

Despite the seeming ubiquity of disability narratives in country music, overt discussions and representations of disability have been excluded from the genre. This is due in large part to the fact that country music has been shaped by an ableist recording industry that has gone to equally great lengths to erase the music of Black, Latinx, and Indigenous artists. Yet, as previously discussed, country music is not a monolith, but is rather characterized by stylistic mixtures that shift in response to constantly changing market demands.[97] Here we offer the still-developing career of Montero Lamar Hill, professionally known as **"Lil Nas X" (1999–)**, as a case study for exploring both the hybridity of modern country music through the emergence of new subgenres, as well as the intersections of race, sexuality, and disability in country music.

In December 2018, Lil Nas X independently released his single "Old Town Road," which became an instant hit that was featured across social media platforms. The genre-bending song features rapped lyrics exploring cowboy imagery accompanied by banjo and backed by bass. This mixture of country and rap characteristics defied simple labels, which resulted in producers and audience members alike classifying it through a variety of subgenres, such as rap country, southern hip hop country, and country trap. In March 2019, the song was re-released by Columbia records and it immediately made Billboard's cross-genre Hot 100 chart, the Hot Country Songs chart, and the Hot R&B/Hip Hop Songs. Yet, despite its initial popularity among a wide array of audiences, "Old Town Road" was subsequently removed from the Hot Country Songs chart as controversy emerged about the song's genre. Critics argued that the decision to pull "Old Town Road" from country charts was made solely due to the song's lack of "traditional country musical characteristics." Yet, this decision belies a double standard, particularly considering the success of other rap-influenced country songs, such as Jason Aldean's "Dirt Road Anthem."[98] In this way, the song's removal was in keeping with country music's long history of attempting to erase the contributions of Black artists, an argument that many musicians and celebrities made on the artist's behalf. Lil Nas X responded by creating a remix of the song featuring country star Billy Ray Cyrus, which subsequently won Best Pop Duo/Group Performance and Best Music Video at the 2020 Grammy Awards.[99]

Yet, Lil Nas X not only faced racial barriers within the music industry for his being a Black artist performing country music, but also for discussing the impact his racial and sexual identity have had on his mental health. Following the success of "Old Town Road," Lil Nas X came out as gay, stating that he felt it was important for audiences and artists to see gay and Black artists performing their music without being censored by the music industry.[100] These revelations allowed Lil Nas X to use his music and celebrity to flip the script of homophobia and ableism within the music industry.

In an attempt to destigmatize conversations surrounding mental health, Lil Nas X posted a series of videos to TikTok where he discussed his struggle with his sexuality and his resulting experiences of depression and suicidal ideation. In 2021, he was awarded the Suicide Prevention Advocate of the Year Award by the Trevor Project, "a nonprofit dedicated to suicide prevention and crisis intervention for lesbian, gay, bisexual, transgender, queer and questioning young people."[101] Such advocacy is especially important considering that 42% of LGBTQ youth experience mental health problems, and 21% of Black LGBTQ youth attempted suicide in 2021.[102] This statistic, coupled with Lil Nas X's own experiences of marginalization as a Black, gay, and disabled genre-bending artist, demonstrates the importance of understanding how these intersecting identities often lead to compounding experiences of oppression. By unapologetically embracing his identity in public and digital spaces, Lil Nas X is succeeding in "racing," "queering," and "cripping" the music industry. Moreover, he is creating opportunities

Case Studies in Popular Music 107

for individuals with "non-normative" bodyminds to participate in the creation of culture, both in country music and beyond. Though different in many ways, the careers of Hank Williams and Lil Nas X both constitute an opportunity for instructors and students to examine the connection between musical genre and audience identity and to explore how genre blending can challenge and expand representation within musical styles.

Additional Reading/Listening for Students

Williams, Hank. "I'm So Lonesome I Could Cry." *YouTube Video*, 2, no. 47 (May 20, 2018). https://www.youtube.com/watch?v=SBN4tttmKBY.

Williams, Hank Jr. with Michael Bane. *Living Proof: An Autobiography*. New York: G.P. Putnam's Sons, 1979.

X, Lil Nas. "Lil Nas X - Old Town Road (Official Movie) ft. Billy Ray Cyrus." *YouTube Video*, 5, no. 08 (May 17, 2019). https://www.youtube.com/watch?v=w2Ov5jzm3j8.

Hip Hop, Krip-Hop, and Dip Hop

Just as the social model of disability emerged from the civil rights movements of the mid- to late-twentieth century, so too did hip hop. Though often viewed as a musical genre, hip hop is a cultural phenomenon that encompasses not only the musical elements of rapping and DJing (or turntabling), but also graffiti arts (tagging) and break dancing.[103] Hip hop emerged in the Bronx during the 1960s and 1970s and was deeply rooted in identity politics, social consciousness, and Black activism. Since that time, hip hop has become a global phenomenon situated in and inflected by the myriad social, political, and cultural concerns of each locale.[104] Hip hop's emphasis on rhetoric as a vehicle for expression has provided a platform for many artists to share their stories and experiences of marginalization. This centrality of narrative coupled with the spread of hip hop as an expressive medium has led to the emergence of many manifestations and subgenres of hip hop all over the world.

Though there is great diversity within this genre, mainstream hip hop has historically been a predominantly Black, male-dominated space in which heteronormativity and able-bodiedness is prized. As a result, hip hop has been inflected with hypermasculine tendencies encouraged by a society that "lionizes masculinity" while also demonizing men of color. As stated by Derek Iwamoto, "Understandably, young men of color often enter into hypermasculine behaviors to combat the degrading effects of racism on their self-esteem."[105] Mainstream hip hop has thus served as a space for Black artists to address issues of racism and inequality within society, while at the same time reinforcing oppressive structures by equating masculinity with heterosexuality and bodymind normativity. However, in recent years mainstream artists have increasingly begun to defy hypermasculine expectations by sharing their own musical narratives of disability.

Case Studies: Kenrick Lamar, Leroy Moore, and Warren "Wawa" Snipe

Kendrick Lamar is one such artist who has worked to address stereotypes of mental health in hip hop. This is perhaps most evident in his album *To Pimp A Butterfly* (2015).[106] Here Lamar explores his experiences with depression, survivor's guilt, gang violence, and alcoholism.[107] Lamar has become increasingly outspoken about the complex intersections between Black identity, hip hop, and disability and about how his musical output is a reflection of the tensions between "fame, fortune, and loss."[108] Lamar has continued to articulate the intersectional complexities of modern African American life, disability, and identity, and in so doing has made in-roads to destigmatizing divergent bodymind experiences. He has received widespread acclaim for his works, particularly his album *DAMN.*, for which he was awarded the 2018 Pulitzer Prize in Music.

Despite efforts by artists such as Lamar to address ableism and homophobia in the genre, mainstream hip hop still largely excludes people with disabilities. As a result, disabled artists have created new subgenres under the hip hop umbrella specifically designed to address this inequality. One such branch of hip hop that has emerged in recent decades is Krip-Hop. Krip-hop is a subgenre of hip hop that plays on the word "crippled."[109] According to **Leroy F. Moore Jr., (b. 1967)** musician, poet, activist, and founder of Krip-Hop Nation, Krip-Hop artists are reclaiming the word "crippled" as a positive identity:

> We're really using it to reflect on what society has said about us, and using it in an empowering kind of way. And we're also using it in a way that connects to history because there were a couple blues artists that named themselves 'Crippled.' So we're taking it, twisting it, and putting it back out there.[110]

Moore grew up in the Bronx in the 1970s and 1980s during the birth of hip hop.[111] Moore started making his own mixtapes at an early age though he struggled to find acceptance within mainstream hip hop circles due to his cerebral palsy. He was rejected by recording companies who, though they liked his material, declined to sign him because they believed his disability would make him unmarketable.[112] Moore responded by creating Krip-Hop

Nation in 2007, an international organization with a mission of supporting musicians with disabilities and combating ableism in the music industry. Since this time, the organization has spread across the globe, establishing chapters in Germany, Italy, New Zealand, Australia, Brazil, South Africa, and the United Kingdom, and hosting concert tours, festivals, and workshops worldwide. In addition to promoting artists with disabilities, intersectionality is central to Krip-Hop Nation's mission. Thus, the organization prides itself on being an inclusive space for Black, Indigenous, and People of Color (BIPOC), women, and LGBTQIA+ individuals.

Another important subgenre that has emerged in response to the exclusive nature of mainstream hip hop is Dip Hop (Deaf hip hop). As previously discussed in the twentieth century section, while hearing impairment is sometimes viewed as a disability, for those who are culturally Deaf, Deafness constitutes a form of identity that is closely tied to a shared history and language as well as bodily difference. Thus, it is important to note that though Dip Hop and Krip-Hop share many of the same goals and concerns in terms of addressing ableism and inequality in the music industry, the degree to which they identify with the term "disability" differs greatly. For most d/Deaf musicians, being d/Deaf is central to their experience of being in the world and is not considered a form of disability.

Due to generations of being excluded from or made to conform to hearing culture, many members of the Deaf community have rejected any association with non-Deaf culture, including music. In fact, for many years those who attempted to participate in traditional music activities were viewed as being "hearing-minded."[113] However, this started shifting in the early 2000s when Deaf artists began to explore music from a Deaf perspective. Drawing upon the foundations of hip hop, these artists created Dip Hop, which pushed "the limits of what 'hearing' means and broadened music discourse to encompass other sensory realms of the body."[114] Dip Hop combines the rhythmic elements and deep bass beats of hip hop with signed musical expression to create an embodied multisensory musical experience. **Warren "Wawa" Snipe (b. 1971)** was one of the early developers of this genre. In addition to performing, Snipe established his own company, SLYKI (Sign Like You Know It) Entertainment to provide "support for other Deaf artists by teaching them how to promote their work and build their careers."[115] Other Deaf artists, such as Prinz-D, Sho'Roc, Sean Forbes, and Polar Bear, emerged alongside Wawa and collaborated to create the album *Deaf and Loud Underground Volume One*. This album not only brought attention to the work of Deaf musicians but also highlighted the perspective of Black Deaf people, who have routinely been marginalized within both Deaf and African American communities.[116] However, Dip Hop has proven to be an inclusive genre that embraces and promotes both Black musicians, such as Wawa and Prinz-D, as well as white rappers, such as Sean Forbes and Finnish rapper SignMark.

In addition to their careers as performers, many of these artists are also Deaf activists. For instance, Sean Forbes founded D-PAN, Deaf Professional Arts Network, a nonprofit organization designed to make music and music culture accessible to Deaf and hard of hearing audiences.[117] Much like Krip-Hop, Dip Hop has become an international genre, including renowned artists, such as SignMark. In addition to demonstrating the power and diversity of hip hop as a vehicle for human expression, Dip Hop allows students to challenge hearing-centric notions of music, offering them an opportunity to view sound as a communicative phenomenon that extends beyond the ear. Moreover, it provides instructors and students with the opportunity to examine their definitions of music and to consider how expanding understanding of music beyond auditory stimuli is an important component of making musical culture accessible to all.

Additional Reading/Listening for Students

Hub Week. "Krip-Hop Nation: The Crossroads Experience." *YouTube Video* 56, no. 34. March 12, 2018. https://www.youtube.com/watch?v=VsWDwN6GfQk.

"Institute." *Krip Hop Nation: More Than Just Music*. Accessed July 20, 2021 https://kriphopnation.com/krip-hop-institute/.

Maler, Anabel. "Musical Expression Among Deaf and Hearing Song Signers." In *The Oxford Handbook of Music and Disability Studies*, edited by Blake Howe, Stephanie Jensen-Moulton, Neil Lerner, and Joseph Straus, 73–91. New York: Oxford University Press, 2016.

MTV News. "Kendrick Lamar Talks About 'u,' His Depression & Suicidal Thoughts (Pt. 2)|MTV News." *YouTube Video*. 10, no. 39 (April 1, 2015) https://www.youtube.com/watch?v=Hu4Pz9PjoII.

TEDx. "Music+Accessibility=What Matters Next|Sean Forbes|TEDxNASA." *YouTube Video* 6, no. 43. (November 22, 2010). https://www.youtube.com/watch?v=NA94vVzYWFw&t=106s

Conclusion

As discussed throughout this chapter, disability plays an important yet often unexamined role in popular music. The case studies herein are not only designed to offer digestible examples from across popular genres but also allow instructors and students to engage with questions such as, "How do disabled musicians use performance as a way to embody, downplay, or negotiate their impairments?" "How have disabled performers used their music to challenge stigmatizing narratives of disability and how successful have they been?" "In what ways does the music/entertainment industry create disabling environments for performers and how are we as audience members complicit in this?" and "In what ways have disability, Deafness, race, ethnicity, gender, sexuality, and class been co-constructed and represented in popular music?" These lines of inquiry suggest that this chapter may raise more questions than it answers. However, we hope that this curiosity sparks critical discourse around disability, Deafness, intersectionality, and pop music that will provide students with the tools to become conscientious participants in the creation of popular music culture.

Notes

1 George McKay, *Shakin' All Over: Popular Music and Disability* (Ann Arbor, MI: University of Michigan Press, 2013), 1.
2 Julie Netherland, ed., *Critical Perspectives on Addiction* (Bingley, United Kingdom: Emerald Group Publishing Limited, 2012), xii.
3 See Rebecca Bunn, "Conceptualizing Addiction as Disability in Discrimination Law: A Situated Comparison," *Contemporary Drug Problems* 46, no. 1 (2019); Stephanie Dotto and Kristi A. Allain, "Curricular Disorder: Disability Studies, Eating Disorders, and Health and Physical Education in Ontario, Canada," *Thresholds* 41, no. 1 (2020); Geoff, "Destabilizing Disability: Including Addiction for Cross-movement Solidarity," *Knots: An Undergraduate Journal of Disability Studies* 1 (2015); and Stephanie Tierney, "Anorexia: Illuminating Impairment or Dishonourable Disability?" *Disability Studies Quarterly* 22, no. 3 (2002), 58–77.
4 McKay, *Shakin' All Over*, 88.
5 As disability studies scholar Rosemarie Garland-Thompson states, "If staring is the effort to make sense of the inexplicable, to craft a narrative of recognition from incoherence, then the target of staring is often that which seems strange or unfamiliar."
6 Francis Davis, *The History of the Blues: The Roots, The Music, The People* (Boston, MA: Da Capo Press, 2003), 4.
7 Ibid, 2.
8 Joseph Witek, "Blindness as a Rhetorical Trope in Blues Discourse," *Black Music Research Journal* 8, no. 2 (1988), 177–178.
9 Terry Rowden, *The Songs of Blind Folk: African American Musicians and the Cultures of Blindness* (Ann Arbor, MI, University of Michigan Press, 2009), 35.
10 Ibid, 50.
11 Joseph Witek, "Blindness as a Rhetorical Trope in Blues Discourse," *Black Music Research Journal* 8, no. 2 (1988): 192.
12 Rowden, *The Songs of Blind Folk*, 53.
13 Ibid.
14 Robert Santelli, *Big Book of Blues* (New York: Penguin Books, 1993), 241.
15 Rowden, *The Songs of Blind Folk*, 55.
16 Ibid, 56.
17 W.K. McNeil, "Forehand, Blind Mamie," in *Encyclopedia of American Gospel Music*, ed. W.K. McNeil (New York: Routledge, 2010), 129.
18 Michelle R. Scott, *Blues Empress in Black Chattanooga: Bessie Smith and the Emerging Urban South* (Champaign, IL: University of Illinois Press, 2008), 83.

112 Case Studies in Popular Music

19 Paul Oliver, "Smith, Bessie," *Grove Music Online*, (2001).
20 Ibid.
21 Jennifer S. Uglow, Frances Hinton, and Maggy Hendry (eds), "Smith, Bessie," in *The Palgrave MacMillan Dictionary of Women's Biography* (4th edition). (Macmillan Publishers Ltd. Credo Reference, 2005), https://login.pallas2.tcl.sc.edu/login?url=https://search.credoreference.com/content/entry/macdwb/smith_bessie/0?institutionId=6481.
22 Oliver, "Smith," 2001.
23 Daphne A. Brooks, "'This Voice Is Not the One'": Amy Winehouse Sings the Ballad of Sonic Blues(face) Culture," *Women & Performance: A Journal of Feminist Theory* 20, no. 1 (2010): 41.
24 Laura Barton, "Amy Winehouse Sang of a Deeply Feminine Suffering," *The Guardian*, July 26, 2011, https://www.theguardian.com/music/2011/jul/26/amy-winehouse-lyrics.
25 Sasha Frere-Jones, "Amy's Circus: The Strange Power of Junkie Retro Soul," *The New Yorker*, February 25, 2008, https://www.newyorker.com/magazine/2008/03/03/amys-circus.
26 Brooks describes blue(s)face as "a vocal phenomenon pioneered by black *and* white women in the early twentieth century that had a ground-shifting impact on the histories of how we sound race and how we racialize sound in the contemporary popular imaginary." Brooks, "This Voice Which Is Not the One'": Amy Winehouse sings the ballad of sonic blue(s) face culture," 49.
27 Brooks, "This Voice Which Is Not the One,'" 49.
28 Ibid, 47.
29 Sally Satel, "Amy Winehouse's Killers," *The Washington Street Journal*, July 27, 2011.
30 The term the "27 Club" originated after the death of Kurt Cobain in 1994. Fans began drawing parallels between Cobain's death and that of other popular music stars who also died at the age of 27, including Robert Johnson, Jimi Hendrix, Jim Morrison, Brian Jones, and Janis Joplin.
31 McKay, *Shakin' All Over*, 152.
32 Ken Burns and Geoffrey C. Ward, *Ken Burns' Jazz: The Story of America's Music* (New York: Sony Music Entertainment, 2000).
33 See Steven Feld, *Jazz Cosmopolitanism in Accra: Five Musical Years in Ghana* (Durham, NC: Duke University Press, 2012); Charles B. Hersch, *Jews and Jazz: Improvising Ethnicity* (London: Routledge, 2016); Bruce Johnson, *Jazz Diaspora: Music and Globalisation* (London: Routledge, 2019); and Andrew Robson, *Austral Jazz: The Localization of a Global Music Form in Sydney* (London: Routledge, 2019).
34 Laurie Stras, "Sing a Song of Difference: Connie Boswell and a Discourse of Disability in Jazz," *Popular Music* 28, no. 3 (2009): 300.
35 Stras, "Sing a Song of Difference," 301.
36 Sean Murray, "That 'Weird and Wonderful Posture': Jump 'Jim Crow' and the Performance of Disability," in *The Oxford Handbook of Music and Disability Studies*, eds. Blake Howe, Stephanie Jensen-Moulton, Neil Lerner, and Joseph Straus (New York: Oxford University Press, 2015), 357–370.
37 Laurie Stras, "White Face, Black Voice: Race, Gender, and Region in the Music of the Boswell Sisters," *Journal of the Society for American Music* 1, no. 2 (2007): 227.
38 Stras, "White Face, Black Voice," 243–244.

39 Stras, "Sing a Song of Difference," 298.
40 Ibid, 249.
41 Ibid, 298.
42 Rowden, *The Songs of Blind Folk*, 86.
43 Ibid, 85.
44 Jeffrey J. Martin, "Supercrip Identity," in *Handbook of Disability Sport and Exercise Psychology* (Oxford Scholarship Online, 2017), https://doi.org/10.1093/oso/9780190638054.003.0015.
45 Rowden, *The Songs of Blind Folk*, 85.
46 Felicity Howlett and J. Bradford Robinson, "Tatum, Art(hur)," *Grove Music Online* (2001), https://doi.org/10.1093/gmo/9781561592630.article.27553.
47 Rowden, *The Songs of Blind Folk*, 87.
48 Howlett and Robinson. "Tatum, Art(hur)."
49 Rowden, *The Songs of Blind Folk*, 89.
50 Howlett and Robinson. "Tatum, Art(hur)."
51 Manouche refers to the French-speaking Romani Tribe that settled in Belgium, Holland, Germany, and the Alsace region of northern France. It is important to address the inclusion of the word "Gypsy" in the context of Reinhardt. To the Roma, the term is considered a racial slur due to its negative connotations of nomadism and vagrancy. While the term "Gypsy" is problematic, in this section we use it in reference to the subgenre of Gypsy jazz (also referred to as Gypsy swing, Manouche jazz, or Manouche swing).
52 This also brings to mind the difficulty among scholars in pinpointing the origins of Reinhardt's musical style, which veered from the traditional Gypsy jazz style by incorporating greater improvisation. Was it Gypsy jazz or at the very least, Roma-influenced? Was it impacted by American jazz and its dominant African musical components? Or was it something entirely his own?
53 Michael H. Kater, *Different Drummers: Jazz in the Culture of Nazi Germany* (New York: Oxford University Press, 2003), 30.
54 For detailed case studies, see George McKay's *Shakin' All Over: Popular Music and Disability*.
55 Stuart A. Kallen, *The History of R & B and Soul Music* (New York: Greenhaven Publishing LLC., 2013), 9.
56 See Terry Rowden's "Blindness and the Rhetoric of 'Genius'" in *The Songs of Blind Folk*.
57 Ibid, 44.
58 Rowden, *The Songs of Blind Folk*, 97.
59 Ray Charles and David Ritz, *Brother Ray: Ray Charles' Own Story,* (New York: Warner Books, 1978).
60 We intentionally omitted a case study of Stevie Wonder as there is already a significant amount of resources on him, the intersectionality of his Blackness and blindness, and how that relates to music (see Will Fulton's chapter "Stevie Wonder's Tactile Keyboard Mediation, Black Key Compositional Development, and the Quest for Creative Autonomy" in *The Oxford Handbook of Music and Disability Studies*).
61 Teddy Pendergrass, "My Biography," *Teddy and Joan Pendergrass Foundation* (2018), https://teddypendergrassofficial.com/teddy-pendergrass-biography/.
62 Pendergrass, "My Biography."
63 McKay, *Shakin' All Over*, 95.

64 Ibid.
65 Pendergrass, "My Biography."
66 Teddy Pendergrass with Patricia Romanowski, *Truly Blessed* (New York: Putnam, 1998), 231.
67 Pendergrass, *Truly Blessed*, 290.
68 Katherine Grennell, "The Making of the 'Fame Monster': Disability Aesthetics, Bodily Deviance, and Celebrity Culture" (PhD diss., University at Buffalo, 2016), 79.
69 As seen in the off-Broadway show *Saving Britney*, Netflix's documentary "Britney Vs. Spears," and Hulu's documentary "Framing Britney Spears."
70 Anastasia Tsioulcas, "Britney Spears' Conservatorship Has Finally Ended," *National Public Radio*, November 12, 2021, https://www.npr.org/2021/11/12/1054860726/britney-spears-conservatorship-ended.
71 The control of reproduction through forced use of birth control is another example of eugenics as well as the misogynistic undercurrents that often disproportionately marginalize disabled women.
72 Bradley Lewis, "A Mad Fight: Psychiatry and Disability Activism," in *The Disability Studies Reader*, 4th edition, ed. Lennard Davis (New York: Routledge, 2013), 116.
73 Ibid.
74 Grennell, "The Making of the Fame Monster," 90.
75 Around 2009–2010, Gaga teamed up with renowned photographer David LaChappelle and released three photos entitled the Lady Gaga Disability Project. Each photo included various themes of disability. Adverse reactions from these photos erupted from academics and the disability community for their fetishization and sensationalism of disability.
76 Christopher R. Smit, "Body Vandalism: Lady Gaga, Disability, and Popular Culture," *Review of Disability Studies* 10, no. 2 (2014): 6.
77 J. Jack Halberstam, *Gaga Feminism: Sex, Gender, and the End of Normal* (Boston, MA: Beacon Press, 2012), xii.
78 Grennell, "The Making of the Fame Monster," 116–117.
79 Katie Ellis, *Disability and Popular Culture Focusing Passion, Creating Community and Expressing Defiance* (Farnham, Great Britain: Routledge, 2016), 102.
80 Grennell, "The Making of the Fame Monster," 146.
81 Lady Gaga, Twitter Post, September 12, 2017, 7:49 AM. https://twitter.com/ladygaga/status/907571825294675968?lang=en.
82 Nadine Hubbs, *Rednecks, Queers, and Country Music* (Berkley, CA: University of California Press, 2014), 8.
83 Charles L. Hughes, *Country Soul: Making Music and Making Race in the American South* (Chapel Hill, NC: University of North Carolina Press, 2015), 7.
84 Hubbs, *Rednecks*, 13.
85 Aaron Fox, *Real Country: Music and Language in Working-Class Culture* (Durham, NC: Duke University Press, 2004), ix.
86 Fox, *Real Country*, 28.
87 According to the American Psychological Association, "Lower levels of SES have consistently been correlated with poor health and lower quality of life."
88 Mark Ribowsky, *Hank: The Short Life and Long Country Road of Hand Williams* (New York: Liveright Publishing Corporation, 2017), xiv.

Case Studies in Popular Music   115

89 Though the exact cause of Lon's impairment is unknown, he did experience frequent periods of disorientation and intermittent facial paralysis in addition to what would now be labeled as Post-Trauma Stress Disorder (Ibid, 8).
90 Ibid, 18.
91 "Spina Bifida Occulta," Columbia Neurosurgery, accessed February 7, 2022, https://www.neurosurgery.columbia.edu/patient-care/conditions/spina-bifida-occulta.
92 Patrick Huber, Steve Goodson, and David Anderson, *The Hank Williams Reader* (New York: Oxford University Press, 2014), 5–6.
93 Ibid, 6.
94 Ribowsky, *Hank*, 11.
95 McKay, *Shakin' All Over*, 70.
96 Bill C. Malone, *Country Music U.S.A.*, 2nd revised edition (Austin, TX: University of Texas Press, 2002), 298.
97 Hubbs, *Rednecks*, 8.
98 Elias Leight, "Lil Nas X's 'Old Town Road' Was a Country Hit. Then Country Changed Its Mind," *Rolling Stone*, March 26, 2019, https://www.rollingstone.com/music/music-features/lil-nas-x-old-town-road-810844/.
99 Haleigh Mauro, "The Real Meaning of the 'Old Town Road' Lyrics," *Cosmopolitan*, March 29, 2021, https://www.cosmopolitan.com/entertainment/music/a28497104/old-town-road-lyrics-meaning-lil-nas-x-billy-ray-cyrus/.
100 Rhian Daly, "Lil Nas X Opens Up about Being Gay and Celebrating His Sexuality," *NME*, January 2, 2022, https://www.nme.com/news/music/lil-nas-x-opens-up-coming-out-celebrating-sexuality-3128521.
101 Mark Kennedy, "Lil Nas X Honored for Suicide Prevention, Mental Health Awareness Efforts," *Chicago Sun Times*, September 1, 2021, https://chicago.suntimes.com/2021/9/1/22652416/lil-nas-x-suicide-prevention-trevor-project-mental-health-lgbtq.
102 "National Survey LGBTQ Youth Mental Health 2021," The Trevor Project, 2021, https://www.thetrevorproject.org/survey-2021/?section=SuicideMentalHealth.
103 Marcia Amidon Lüsted and Damon Sajnani, *Hip-Hop Music* (Minneapolis, MN: Essential Library, 2018), 18.
104 For a greater exploration of these intersections see Murray Forman, *The 'Hood Comes First: Race, Space, and Place in Rap and Hip-Hop* (Middletown, CT: Wesleyan University Press, 2002) and Sujatha Fernandes, *Close to the Edge: In Search of the Global Hip Hop Generation* (Sydney, NSW: NewSouth Publishing, 2011).
105 Derek Iwamoto, "Tupac Shakur: Understanding the Identity Formation of a Hyper-Masculinity of Popular Hip-Hop Artist," *Black Scholar* 33, no. 2 (2003): 1231–1251.
106 Kendrick Lamar, *To Pimp a Butterfly* [Album], Top Dawg Entertainment, 2015.
107 Ibid.
108 Rob Markman, "Kendrick Lamar Reveals to Pimp a Butterfly's Original Title and Its Tupac Connection," *MTV News*, March 13, 2015, https://www.google.com/url?q=http://www.mtv.com/news/2120689/kendrick-lamar-tu-pimp-a-caterpillar-tupac/&sa=D&source=docs&ust=1644845850989897&usg=AOvVaw2-t9IlfqMFZQSD23FBGMh0.
109 As stated by Tory V. Pearman in the *Medieval Disability Glossary*, "In Old English, the noun *cripp*le (*crypel, creople, crypol*) is related to the Old Frisian

kreppel Old Norse *kryppill*, and Middle Dutch *cröpel, crepel* and generally refers to a person who is physically disabled by impairment to the limbs." Though still viewed as offensive when used in derogatory contexts, many disability activities have reclaimed this term and the term "crip" as a positive identity.

110 Lisa Hix, "Interview with Leroy Moore, Founder of Krip Hop Nation," *KQED*, February 14, 2011, https://www.kqed.org/arts/43903/interview_with_leroy_moore_founder_of_krip_hop_nation.
111 "About Krip Hop Nation," *Krip Hop Nation: More than Just Music*, accessed July 19, 2021, https://kriphopnation.com/.
112 Hix, "Interview with Leroy Moore, Founder of Krip Hop Nation."
113 The term "hearing-minded" is applied to members of the Deaf community who are deaf but wish to communicate through speech rather than sign language.
114 Katelyn Best, "Musical Belonging in Hearing-Centric Society: Adapting and Contesting Dominant Cultural Norms through Deaf Hip Hop," *Journal of American Sign Languages & Literatures* (2018): 64, http://journalofasl.com/deaf-hiphop/.
115 Katelyn Best, "'We Still Have a Dream': The Deaf Hip Hop Movement and the Struggle against the Socio-Cultural Marginalization of Deaf People," *Song and Popular Culture* 60/61 (2015), 65.
116 Though Gallaudet University, the only Deaf institution of higher learning in the world, was established in 1864, it didn't have its first Black graduate until 1954 following the *Brown v. Board of Education* Supreme Court case (Benro Ogunyipe, "Black Deaf Culture through the Lens of History," *Described and Captioned Media Program*, February 2021, https://dcmp.org/learn/366-black-deaf-culture-through-the-lens-of-history).
117 "Our Mission," D-PAN, accessed July 20, 2021, https://d-pan.org/our-mission/.

References

American Psychological Association. "Disability and Socioeconomic Status." Accessed March 30, 2022. https://www.apa.org/pi/ses/resources/publications/disability.

Barton, Laura. "Amy Winehouse Sang of a Deeply Feminine Suffering." *The Guardian*. July 26, 2011. https://www.theguardian.com/music/2011/jul/26/amy-winehouse-lyrics.

Best, Katelyn. "Musical Belonging in Hearing-Centric Society: Adapting and Contesting Dominant Cultural Norms through Deaf Hip Hop." *Journal of American Sign Languages & Literatures* (2018). Accessed September 12, 2018. http://journalofasl.com/deaf-hiphop/.

———. ""We Still Have a Dream": The Deaf Hip Hop Movement and the Struggle against the Socio-Cultural Marginalization of Deaf People." *Song and Popular Culture* 60/61 (2015): 61–86.

Brooks, Daphne A. "'This Voice Which Is not the One'": Amy Winehouse Sings the Ballad of Sonic Blue(s) Face Culture." *Women & Performance: A Journal of Feminist Theory* 20, no. 1 (2010): 37–60.

Bunn, Rebecca. "Conceptualizing Addiction as Disability in Discrimination Law: A Situated Comparison." *Contemporary Drug Problems* 46, no. 1 (2019): 58–77.

Burns, Ken and Geoffrey C. Ward. *Ken Burns' Jazz: The Story of America's Music*. New York: Sony Music Entertainment, 2000.

Charles, Ray and David Ritz. *Brother Ray: Ray Charles' Own Story*. New York: Warner Books, 1978.

Columbia Neurosurgery. "Spina Bifida Occulta." Accessed February 7, 2022. https://www.neurosurgery.columbia.edu/patient-care/conditions/spina-bifida-occulta.

Daly, Rhian. "Lil Nas X Opens Up about Being Gay and Celebrating His Sexuality." NME. January 2, 2022. https://www.nme.com/news/music/lil-nas-x-opens-up-coming-out-celebrating-sexuality-3128521.

Davis, Francis. *The History of the Blues: The Roots, The Music, The People*. Boston, MA: Da Capo Press, 2003.

Dotto, Stephanie and Kristi A. Allain. "Curricular Disorder: Disability Studies, Eating Disorders, and Health and Physical Education in Ontario, Canada." *Thresholds* 41, no. 1 (2020): 19–32.

D-Pan. "Our Mission." Accessed July 20, 2021 https://d-pan.org/our-mission/.

Ellis, Katie. *Disability and Popular Culture: Focus Passion, Creating Community and Expressing Deviance*. Burlington: Ashgate, 2015.

Feld, Steven. *Jazz Cosmopolitanism in Accra: Five Musical Years in Ghana*. Durham, NC: Duke University Press, 2012.

Fernandes, Sujatha. *Close to the Edge: In Search of the Global Hip Hop Generation*. Sydney, NSW: NewSouth Publishing, 2011.

Forman, Murray. *The 'Hood Comes First: Race, Space, and Place in Rap and Hip-Hop*. Middletown, CT: Wesleyan University Press, 2002.

Fox, Aaron. *Real Country: Music and Language in Working-Class Culture*. Durham, NC: Duke University Press, 2004.

Frere-Jones, Sasha. "Amy's Circus: The Strange Power of Junkie Retro Soul." *The New Yorker*. February 25, 2008. https://www.newyorker.com/magazine/2008/03/03/amys-circus.

Garland-Thomson, Rosemarie. "Staring at the Other." *Disability Studies Quarterly* 25, no. 4 (2005). Accessed October 12, 2021 https://dsq-sds.org/article/view/610/787.

Geoff. "Destabilizing Disability: Including Addiction for Cross-Movement Solidarity." *Knots: An Undergraduate Journal of Disability Studies* 1 (2015): 67–75.

Grennell, Katherine. "The Making of the "Fame Monster": Disability Aesthetics, Bodily Deviance, and Celebrity Culture." PhD diss., University at Buffalo, 2016.

Halberstam, J. Jack. *Gaga Feminism: Sex, Gender, and the End of Normal*. Boston, MA: Beacon Press, 2012.

Hersch, Charles B. *Jews and Jazz: Improvising Ethnicity*. London: Routledge, 2016.

Hix, Lisa. "Interview with Leroy Moore, Founder of Krip Hop Nation." *KQED*. Accessed July 19, 2021. https://www.kqed.org/arts/43903/interview_with_leroy_moore_founder_of_krip_hop_nation.

Howlett, Felicity and J. Bradford Robinson. "Tatum, Art(hur)." *Grove Music Online*. Accessed October 11, 2021. https://doi.org/10.1093/gmo/9781561592630.article.27553.

Hubbs, Nadine. *Rednecks, Queers, and Country Music*. Berkeley, CA: University of California Press, 2014.

Huber, Patrick, Steve Goodson, and David Anderson. *The Hank Williams Reader*. New York: Oxford University Press, 2014.

Hughes, Charles L. *Country Soul: Making Music and Making Race in the American South*. Chapel Hill, NC: University of North Carolina Press, 2015.

Iwamoto, Derek. "Tupac Shakur: Understanding the Identity Formation of a Hyper-Masculinity of Popular Hip-Hop Artist," *Black Scholar* 33, no. 2 (2003): 1231–1251.

Johnson, Bruce. *Jazz Diaspora: Music and Globalisation*. London: Routledge, 2019.

Kallen, Stuart A. *The History of R & B and Soul Music*. New York: Greenhaven Publishing LLC, 2013.

Kater, Michael H. *Different Drummers: Jazz in the Culture of Nazi Germany*. New York: Oxford University Press, 2003.

Kennedy, Mark. "Lil Nas X Honored for Suicide Prevention, Mental Health Awareness Efforts." *Chicago Sun Times*. September 1, 2021. https://chicago.suntimes.com/2021/9/1/22652416/lil-nas-x-suicide-prevention-trevor-project-mental-health-lgbtq.

Krip Hop Nation: More than Just Music. "About Krip Hop Nation." Accessed July 19, 2021. https://kriphopnation.com/.

Lady Gaga (@LadyGaga). "In Our Documentary the #Chronicillness #Chronicpain I Deal w/ is #Fibromyalgia I Wish to Help Raise Awareness & Connect People Who Have it." *Twitter*, September 12, 2017. https://twitter.com/ladygaga/status/907571825294675968?lang=en.

Lamar, Kendrick. *To Pimp a Butterfly [Album]*. Top Dawg Entertainment, 2015.

Leight, Elias. "Lil Nas X's "Old Town Road" Was a Country Hit. Then Country Changed Its Mind." *Rolling Stone*. March 26, 2019. https://www.rollingstone.com/music/music-features/lil-nas-x-old-town-road-810844/.

Lewis, Bradley. "A Mad Fight: Psychiatry and Disability Activism." In *The Disability Studies Reader*, edited by Lennard Davis, 4th edition. New York: Routledge, 2013: 115–131.

Lüsted, Marcia Amidon. *Hip-Hop Music*. Minneapolis, MN: ABDO Publishing Company, 2017.

Malone, Bill C. *Country Music U.S.A.* 2nd revised edition. Austin, TX: University of Texas Press, 2002.

Markman, Rob. "Kendrick Lamar Reveals to Pimp a Butterfly's Original Title and Its Tupac Connection." *MTV News*. March 13, 2015. https://www.google.com/url?q=http://www.mtv.com/news/2120689/kendrick-lamar-tu-pimp-a-caterpillar-tupac/&sa=D&source=docs&ust=1644845850989897&usg=AOvVaw2-t9IlfqMFZQSD23FBGMh0.

Martin, Jeffrey J. "Supercrip Identity." In *Handbook of Disability Sport and Exercise Psychology*. Oxford University Press. 2017. https://oxford.universitypressscholarship.com/view/10.1093/oso/9780190638054.001.0001/oso-9780190638054-chapter-15.

Mauro, Haleigh. "The Real Meaning of the "Old Town Road" Lyrics." *Cosmopolitan*. March 29, 2021. https://www.cosmopolitan.com/entertainment/music/a28497104/old-town-road-lyrics-meaning-lil-nas-x-billy-ray-cyrus/.

McKay, George. *Shakin' All Over. Popular Music and Disability*. Ann Arbor: University of Michigan Press, 2013.
McNeil, W.K. "Forehand, Blind Mamie." In *Encyclopedia of American Gospel Music*, edited by W.K. McNeil. New York: Routledge, 2010.
Murray, Sean. "That "Weird and Wonderful Posture": Jump "Jim Crow" and the Performance of Disability." In *The Oxford Handbook of Music and Disability Studies*, edited by Blake Howe, Stephanie Jensen-Moulton, Neil Lerner, and Joseph Straus, 357–370. New York: Oxford University Press, 2015.
Netherland, Julie, Ed. *Critical Perspectives on Addiction*. Bingley, United Kingdom: Emerald Group Publishing Limited, 2012.
Ogunyipe, Benro, "Black Deaf Culture Through the Lens of History." *Described and Captioned Media Program*. February 2021. https://dcmp.org/learn/366-black-deaf-culture-through-the-lens-of-history.
Oliver, Paul. "Smith, Bessie." Grove Music Online. Accessed September 14, 2021. https://doi.org/10.1093/gmo/9781561592630.article.26000.
Pearman, Tory V. "Cripple." *Medieval Disability Glossary*. Accessed March 30, 2022. https://medievaldisabilityglossary.hcommons.org/cripple/.
Pendergrass, Teddy. "My Biography." Teddy and Joan Pendergrass Foundation. Accessed October 18, 2021 https://teddypendergrassofficial.com/teddy-pendergrass-biography/.
———. *Truly Blessed*. With Patricia Romanowski. New York: Putnam, 1998.
Ribowsky, Mark. *Hank: The Short Life and Long Country Road of Hand Williams*. New York: Liveright Publishing Corporation, 2017.
Robson, Andrew. *Austral Jazz: The Localization of a Global Music Form in Sydney*. London: Routledge, 2019.
Rowden, Terry. *The Songs of Blind Folk: African American Musicians and the Cultures of Blindness*. Ann Arbor, MI: University of Michigan Press, 2009.
Santelli, Robert. *Big Book of Blues*. New York: Penguin Books, 1993.
Satel, Sally. "Amy Winehouse's Killers." *WSJ*. July 27, 2011. https://www.wsj.com/articles/SB10001424053111903999904576470080054135712.
Scott, Michelle R. *Blues Empress in Black Chattanooga: Bessie Smith and the Emerging Urban South*. Champaign, IL: University of Illinois Press, 2008.
Smit, Christopher R. "Body Vandalism: Lady Gaga, Disability, and Popular Culture." *Review of Disability Studies* 10, no. 2 (2014). https://www.rdsjournal.org/index.php/journal/article/view/31/118.
Stras, Laurie. "Sing a Song of Difference: Connie Boswell and a Discourse of Disability in Jazz." *Popular Music* 28, no. 3 (2009): 297–332.
———. "White Face, Black Voice: Race, Gender, and Region in the Music of the Boswell Sisters." *Journal of the Society for American Music* 1, no. 2 (2007): 207–255.
"The 27 Club: A Brief History: From Robert Johnson to Anton Yelchin, 20 Stars Who Died at 27." *Rolling Stone*. Accessed September 28, 2021. https://www.rollingstone.com/culture/culture-lists/the-27-club-a-brief-history-17853/robert-johnson-26971/.
The Trevor Project. "National Survey LGBTQ Youth Mental Health 2021." 2021. https://www.thetrevorproject.org/survey-2021/?section=SuicideMentalHealth.

Tierney, Stephanie. "Anorexia: Illuminating Impairment or Dishonourable Disability?" *Disability Studies Quarterly* 22, no. 3 (2002): https://dsq-sds.org/article/view/356/459.

Tsioulcas, Anastasia. "Britney Spears' Conservatorship Has Finally Ended." *National Public Radio*, November 12, 2021. https://www.npr.org/2021/11/12/1054860726/britney-spears-conservatorship-ended.

Uglow, Jennifer S., Frances Hinton, and Maggy Hendry (eds). "Smith, Bessie." In *The Palgrave MacMillan Dictionary of Women's Biography*, 4th edition. Macmillan Publishers Ltd. Credo Reference, 2005. https://login.pallas2.tcl.sc.edu/login?url=https://search.credoreference.com/content/entry/macdwb/smith_bessie/0?institutionId=6481.

Witek, Joseph. "Blindness as a Rhetorical Trope in Blues Discourse." *Black Music Research Journal* 8, no. 2 (1988): 177–193.

Conclusion
Where Do We Go from Here?

Though this text provides an overview of music and disability studies, offers suggestions for practical applications in course design and implementation, and shares case studies from both the Western Art Music canon and popular music genres, we understand this is only a limited snapshot of disability accessibility as it relates to the music classroom. We envision this as an open-ended, constantly evolving dialogue that will shift over time with the needs of our students. It is thus incumbent upon us as educators to continue to engage in these conversations and to imagine and re-imagine how we might make our music classrooms accessible for all students. In these last pages, we would like to offer one final reflection on the place of accommodation and accessibility in music.

Higher education makes many demands of its instructors: we must adopt new teaching approaches, increase retention efforts, and engage in institutional initiatives centered around diversity, equity, inclusion, and belonging (DEIB). Each of these is important and crucial to building a healthy learning environment and institutional culture. However, at times these concepts are tokenized at the expense of outward displays of performative DEIB policies. In these instances, such initiatives often become the newest and shiniest project that occupy the full attention of institutions (either in word and deed or sometimes only the former) until the problem is seemingly "fixed." Accessibility and inclusivity have occupied this space as "buzzwords" before and will likely do so again in the future. However, in the world we envision for ourselves and our students, accessibility and inclusivity are not institutional "fads" or an issue of legal compliance. They are a fundamental human right for which we are all responsible. In this way, accessible and inclusive education is about cultivating a culture of care that both enables and empowers learners to succeed. Implementing policies that ensure the equity and protection of all people in academic environments is essential. Yet, equally important is the work that we as instructors do in the classroom. This is often where small but powerful changes take place through the exchange of ideas and dialogue about the historical and current role of music in expressing, shaping, and changing culture.

But where do we go from here? Though limited in scope, we hope that this text will assist instructors in implementing accessibility efforts in their classrooms and curricula and, perhaps more importantly, will spark new efforts to further inclusivity and accommodation in musical pedagogy. Notably missing from this text are the voices of Black, Brown, Indigenous, and transgender disabled music educators as well as the thoughts and perspectives of disabled students. Furthermore, the perspectives of the current authors represent only two narratives of disability. There is also a need to incorporate input from scholars and pedagogues in the disability community more broadly. If we are to realize our goal of inclusion, then we must create a welcoming environment in which these voices are invited into conversations about music, history, and culture. Accessibility is only truly possible through inclusion.

There are numerous works dedicated to exploring disability and music through case studies of specific artists, genres, and traditions, many of which are cited throughout this text. However, at the time of this writing, there are no exhaustive histories of music and disability. Therefore, we hope that this book serves as a beginning for collating narratives of disabled composers and case studies of disability in music into a true history of disability in music. Though an ambitious undertaking, we envision a resource similar in scope to that of the *Grove Music Online* for disability. Such a project would facilitate collaboration from scholars across music disciplines around the globe, allowing intersectional voices to contribute their experience and expertise and, in so doing, ensure a diversity of disabled and Deaf perspectives. Moreover, this resource would create a repository of disability music history for generations to come, effectively bringing disabled scholars and musicians out of the margins. The mere existence of such a resource would be revolutionary in demonstrating the importance and ubiquity of disability in musical culture writ large. It is our hope that *Disability and Accessibility in the Music Classroom: A Teacher's Guide* will serve as a point of departure for such a project.

Though music history is often presented as a fixed entity, as evidenced from this text, we are constantly re-discovering musical narratives that have previously been excluded. As instructors, we have a unique opportunity to uncover these perspectives with our students and to demonstrate that far from studying a monolithic music history, we are in fact exploring multilayered, intersectional music histories. Though disability has been largely ignored in these histories, it is present in the music we study and is experienced by our colleagues, our students, and even ourselves. As music history instructors, it is our responsibility to explore these histories and experiences in our classrooms and curricula. It is only through this centering of marginalized voices that we will be able to truly cultivate a lasting culture of accessibility and inclusivity in the music classroom.

Index

ableism xiii, 10, 22, 67
accessibility xiii–xiv, 10, 13–14, 32, 121–123
accessibility checkers 23–26
accessibility office *see* Student Disability Resource Center (SCRC)
Accessible Music Technology (AMT) 37
accommodations office *see* Student Disability Resource Center (SCRC)
addiction 89, 97, 105
Adobe Acrobat Pro Accessibility Checker 24–26
alcoholism 89–90, 103
Americans with Disabilities Act (ADA) xiii, 8–9, 12–13, 22–23
Americans with Disabilities Amendments Act of 2008 (ADAAA) xiii, 13
anxiety and depression 98
Artusi, Giovanni 56
assessment 26–29
the average man (l'homme moyen) 65

Bach, J. S. (Johann Sebastian) 57, 58
Baroque period 55–60, 62, 63
Bassler, Samantha 52
Baynton, Douglas 2
Beethoven, Ludwig van 66–68, 70; "Eroica" Symphony 67; *Heiligenstadt Testament* 67
Bingen, Hildegarde von 47–49; *Ordo virtutum (Order of the Virtues)* 48–49; *Scivias (Know the Ways of the Lord)* 48–49

bipolar disorder 98–99
Black, Indigenous, and People of Color (BIPOC) xiii, 32, 109
Black people 87–90, 92–93, 97–99, 102, 105–109
blindness 49–51, 57, 87–89, 93–94, 97
Blue Notes 97; "If You Don't Know Me By Now" 97; "The Love I Lost" 97; "Wake Up Everybody" 97
the blues 87–91
bodyminds: accessibility 10, 107; definition xiii; and enfreakment 72; and music 52, 108; and perceptions of 60–61, 65–66, 70
Boethius 52–53; *De institutione musica* 52
Boswell, Connie 92–93
The Boswell Sisters 92–93
Braille, Louis 66
Broschi, Carlo *see* Farinelli
Burton, Robert 54

Calderone, Jo *see* Lady Gaga
Castiglione, Baldassare 52, 55; *Book of the Courtier* 55
castrati 58–62, 64
Catholic Church 47, 58–59, 62
Center for Teaching and Learning xiii, 34
cerebral palsy 108
Charles, Ray 96–97; *Brother Ray* 97
Christianity 47; *see also* Catholic Church
chronic illness 49, 57–58, 68–69, 73
Classical Era 55, 60–65

126 *Index*

Convention of the Rights of Persons with Disabilities (CRPD) xiii, 13
country music 101–107
Crawford, Katherine 59
Crenshaw, Kimberlé 11
cultural disabilities studies xiii, 11–12
Cyrus, Billy Ray 106

Dap-Kings 90
Daverio, John 69
Davis, Francis 87
d/Deaf xiii, 67, 74, 109
Deaf and Loud Underground Volume One 109
deafness 66–68, 74
Deaf studies 45–46
Deaville, James 69
Differentiated Instruction (DI) xiv
dip hop 109–110
disability: cultural disabilities studies xiii, 11–12; and definition xiv, 8–10, 12; disability rights 70; disability studies xiv, 2, 5, 9–12, 45–46, 60, 69; and disclosure 14; and exclusion 2; as inspiration 47, 68; narratives of 4–5, 98; perceptions of 46–47, 61; performance of 60, 86–87, 91; as punishment 47, 49, 60; representation 93, 100; *see also* models of disability
Disability Rights Movement xiv, 2, 4, 11–13, 70
disablism xiv, 10–11
diversity, equity, inclusion, and belonging (DEIB) xiv, 2, 121
Doctrine of Affections 56, 63
Doctrine of Ethos 56
Dolmage, Jay 22
Dowland, John 54; *Flow my tears* 54; *Lachrimae* (or *Seaven Teares Figured in Seaven Passionate Pavans*) 54; *Melancholy Gailliard* 54
D-PAN (Deaf Professional Arts Network) 110

Education for all Handicapped Children Act of 1975 xiv, 12
Ellinwood, Leonard 49–50; *The Works of Francesco Landini* 49–50
Emens, Elizabeth 13

"Empress of Blues" *see* Smith, Bessie
enfreakment 72–73, 100
Enlightenment period 55, 60–62, 64
eugenics xiv, 65, 67, 70

Farinelli 59
fibromyalgia 100
Ficino, Marsilio 52
504 Sit-Ins 12
Forbes, Sean 110
Forehand, Blind Mamie 89
Fox, Aaron 102
Frere-Jones, Sasha 90

Galton, Sir Francis 65
Garland-Thomson, Rosemarie 11–12
genius 69, 87, 94, 97
Genius of Soul *see* Charles, Ray
Germanotta, Steffani *see* Lady Gaga
Glennie, Evelyn 72, 74; *Listen World!* 74
Gluck, Christoph 62; *Orfeo ed Euridice* 62
Gordon, Bernard 54
Grove, Floyd 63

Handel, George Frideric 57–59; *Giulio Cesare* 57; *Messiah* 57
Haydn, Franz Joseph 61–64; Andante o più tosto ("Razor" quartet, Op. 55 No. 2) 63–64; Fürnberg quartets 63; "Razor" quartet, Op. 55 No. 2 63–64
"hearing-minded" 109
Hildegarde, Saint *see* Bingen, Hildegarde von
Hill, Montero Lamar *see* Lil Nas X
"Hillbilly Shakespeare" or "Hillbilly King" *see* Williams, Hiram "Hank"
hip hop 107–108
homosexuality 106
Howlett, Felicity 94
Hubb, Nadine 101–102; *Rednecks, Queers, and Country Music* 101
humanism 51–52, 56
humors: humoral model of medicine 52, 56–57, 61; and music 53–54

identity 4, 73–74, 95, 100–101
illness *see* chronic illness

impairment: definition xiv; and disability 9–10, 61, 71; and the ideal 61, 65; and models of disability 46–47, 57–58, 60; and music 62–64; perceptions of 46–47, 50, 60, 66–68, 100
inclusion and inclusivity xiv, 1–2, 8, 13–15, 121–123
Individuals with Disabilities Education Act (IDEA) xiv, 12–13
intersectionality xiv, 2, 11, 55
Iwamoto, Derek 107

jazz 91–96
Jefferson, Blind Lemon 88–89

krip hop 108–109
Krip-Hop Nation 108–109

Lady Gaga 100–101; "Born this Way" 100; *Born This Way Ball* 100; "Paparazzi" 100
Lady Gaga Disability Project 100
Lamar, Kendrick 108; *DAMN.* 108; *To Pimp A Butterfly* 108
Landini, Francesco 49–51; "Non avrá má pieta" 50
"Landini cadence" 50
Law, Hedy 62; "A Cannon-Shaped Man with an Amphibian Voice" 62
"law or error" 65
Lewis, Bradley 99
l'homme moyen (the average man) 65
Lil Nas X 105–107; "Old Town Road" 105–106
Lorde, Audre 2

madness xiv–xv, 68–69
Mad Pride Movement xv, 79–86, 99
McKay, George 86, 90–91, 104
medical model of disability xv, 9–10, 12, 47, 65–71, 73, 91–92
medieval Christianity 47
melancholia 54–55
mental health xv, 66–69, 90, 98–99, 106, 108
Meyer, Anne 21
Microsoft Accessibility Checker 23–24
Middle Ages 46–52
models of disability: medical model xv, 9–10, 12, 47, 65–71, 73, 91–92;

Index 127

proto-medical model 52, 56–58, 61; rehabilitative xv, 9; religious or moral 47, 52, 60–61; social model of disability xv, 10, 68, 70–71, 73, 74
modernism 71, 72
Monteverdi, Claudio 54; "Cruda Amarilli" 56; *L'Orfeo* 54, 56
Moore, Leroy F. Jr. 108–109
Moore, Shelley 1, 20
music: and disability 71, 73, 104; and emotions 63; and human behavior 52, 56; and medicine 52–54; and sonic pathology 91–92

natural or naturalness 60–64
New Musicology 45
"normal" or "norm" 65, 69
normative xv, 69, 73, 107, 108
Novak, Katie 21

Ōe, Kenzaburō 45
Open Educational Resources (OER) xv, 34
others and othering 55, 59, 62, 64, 92–93
overcoming narrative 94–95, 97

paraplegia 98
Pearson, Karl 65
Pendergrass, Teddy 97–98; *Truly Blessed* 98
performative identity 100–101; *see also* identity
Peri, Jacopo 56; *L'Euridice* 56
person-first language 4
Picker, Tobias 72
polio 92
pop music 98–101
proto-medical model of disability 52, 56–58, 61
psychology 66, 69
Purcell, Henry 54; *Dido and Aeneas* 54

Quetelet, Adolphe 65

Ramos de Pareja, Bartolomeo 53–54; *Musica Practica* 53–54
Rehabilitation Act of 1973 xv, 12, 22
rehabilitative model of disability xv, 9
Reinhardt, Jean "Django" 94–95

Renaissance era 51–55, 58
rheumatism 57
rhythm and blues 96–98
Rinuccini, Cino 51
Robinson, J. Bradford 94
Robinson, Ray Charles *see* Charles, Ray
rock and roll 96–98
Romantic Era 65–70
Rose, David 21
Rowden, Terry 87–88, 97

Sacks, Oliver 49
Schoenberg, Arnold 72–73; Fourth Spring Quartet (Op. 37) 73; Piano Suite (Op. 25) 73; *Pierrot Lunaire* 72; String Trio 73; Third Spring Quartet (Op. 30) 73; Violin Concerto (Op. 36) 73
Schumann, Clara 69
Schumann, Robert 68–70
screen reader xv
Section 504 xv, 12
Section 508 xv, 12, 22
Sensory Processing Disorder (SPD) 37–38
sexuality 98, 106
Siebers, Tobin 1, 9
Sign Like You Know It (SLYKI) Entertainment 109
Singer, Charles 49
Sins Invalid 11; "10 Principles of Disability Justice" 11
sit-ins 12
Smit, Christopher R. 99
Smith, Bessie 89–91; *Downhearted Blues* 89; "Gimme a Pigfoot and a Bottle of Beer" 89; "Gin House Blues" 89–90; "Me and My Gin" 89, 91
Snipe, Warren "Wawa"" 109
social model of disability xv, 10, 68, 70–71, 73, 74
Spears, Brittney 98–100; "Baby one more time" 98
Special Education 4
spina bifida occulta 103, 105
Squarcialupi Codex 50

staring 87
stigma 14, 62
Stras, Laurie 91, 93
Straus, Joseph 69; *Extraordinary Measures* 69
Stravinsky, Igor 72–73; Piano Sonata 73; *The Rake's Progress* 73; *Requiem Canticles* 73; *The Rite of Spring* 72; Symphony in C 73
Strozzi, Barbara 56; "Lagrime mie" 56
Student Disability Resource Center (SCRC) xv, 14, 33

Tatum, Arthur (Art) 94
Taylor, "Chevalier" John 58
"tear motive" 54
Tråvén, Marianne 62
Twentieth Century 70–75

Universal Design for Learning (UDL) xv, 20–22
Universal Design in Education, Universal Design of Instruction *see* Universal Design for Learning (UDL)

Web Content Accessibility Guidelines (WCAG) xv, 22–23
Wendell, Susan 10
Western Art Music Canon (WAM) xv, 45–46
Wheatley, Edward 47
Williams, Hank Jr. 104–105; "Family Tradition" 104–105
Williams, Hiram "Hank" 103–105; "Cold Cold Heart" 103; "I'm So Lonesome I Could Cry" 103; "Your Cheatin' Heart" 103
Winehouse, Amy 90–91; *Back to Black* 90; "Rehab" 91
working-class 102, 104
WWI (1914-1918) 70–73
WWII (1939-1945) 71, 95

Yüyi *see* Lady Gaga

Zarlino, Gioseffe 53–55; *Le institutioni harmoniche* 53

For Product Safety Concerns and Information please contact our EU representative GPSR@taylorandfrancis.com
Taylor & Francis Verlag GmbH, Kaufingerstraße 24, 80331 München, Germany

www.ingramcontent.com/pod-product-compliance
Lightning Source LLC
Chambersburg PA
CBHW051751230426
43670CB00012B/2240